Rights in Moral Lives

Rights in Moral Lives

A Historical-Philosophical Essay

A. I. Melden

UNIVERSITY OF CALIFORNIA PRESS

Berkeley / Los Angeles / London

BJ
1031
. M38
1988
Crp. 2

University of California Press
Berkeley and Los Angeles, California

University of California Press, Ltd.
London, England

Copyright ©1988 by A. I. Melden

Library of Congress Cataloging-in-Publication Data

Melden, A. I. (Abraham Irving), 1910–
    Rights in moral lives : a historical-philosophical essay /
A. I. Melden.
    p.   cm
    Includes bibliographical references and index.
    ISBN 0-520-06275-2 (alk. paper)
    1. Ethics.   I. Title.
BJ1031.M38 1988
172'.2—dc19

87-34234
CIP

Printed in the United States of America

1   2   3   4   5   6   7   8   9

For Rege

Contents

Preface   ix

1. Rights in Ancient Thought?   1
2. Modern Conceptions of Rights   6
3. Rights—Pro and Con   13
4. Mill on Rights   15
5. Human or Fundamental Rights   39
6. Animal Rights?   51
7. Analysis or Change?   73
8. Moral Progress   90
9. Solutions?   119
10. Conclusions   138

Index   151

Preface

Those of us who have recognized the importance of moral rights must at some time or other have asked ourselves the question whether the ancients, especially the Greeks, had any notion of a moral right. For no mention of such rights is to be found in the writings of the ancient moralists, even when they concern questions about justice. But the ways in which this question about rights in antiquity has been discussed in the literature have dissatisfied me for quite some time. For when writers have addressed this question, they have ignored important conceptual issues, contenting themselves with little more than a review of the sorts of words or expressions that the ancients employed in situations in which *we*, with *our* moral vocabulary, would have employed the language of rights. And not infrequently the question has been put in a way that implies or at least suggests that if the ancients did indeed have *some* notion of a moral right, they must have had *the* concept of moral right in mind. This ignores the fact that talk about rights has undergone substantial changes ever since its first appearance in early modern times, a fact that clearly raises the question whether the changes that have occurred are no mere changes in the analyses that writers have offered of "the" concept of a right—a concept that somehow came full-blown into existence in the early modern period—but changes in the concepts themselves.

It is for this reason that I have examined in this essay the views of certain major historical figures. These views are frequently misunderstood, as in the case of John Locke, or unfortunately ignored despite their considerable importance as in the case of John Stuart Mill, whose account of rights in the fifth chapter of *Utilitarianism* is by no means transparently clear. In the course of this historical study I have also discussed developments that have occurred in very recent years. Against this background I have expressed my own ideas—on certain matters, my second thoughts—before raising certain conceptual or philosophical issues to which we must address ourselves if we are to deal satisfactorily with what has generally been taken to be a question of simple historical fact, the question whether the ancients had any notion of a moral right.

I have benefited from discussions with Professor Gerasimos Santas and from the comments of Professor Allen Buchanan on a draft of this essay; and I have been most fortunate in having had the assistance of Nancy Atkinson, copy editor for the Univerity of California Press in bringing the manuscript of this essay into its final form.

1. Rights in Ancient Thought?

Those of us who have been concerned to emphasize the importance of rights in our moral thinking have wondered on occasion whether the ancients, specifically the Greeks, had any notion of a right, some idea of the moral property of agents—subjective rights as the continentals label them—as distinct from the moral property of actions. And the answer that some have given, *tout court*, is that the ancients do not appear to have any such idea.

The reasons for this view are simple. Plato and Aristotle, to mention only two examples, engage in extensive discussions of the nature of justice, a notion to which, as Mill later pointed out, the concept of rights is of central importance; but no such idea is so much as mentioned in their discussions of justice and the various forms of injustice. And as scholars familiar with the relevant texts inform us, there is no word in Greek or in Latin that functions as the equivalent of the word we use to mark the moral property of agents. From this it has been concluded, not infrequently, that the concept of a right is a late addition to our moral thinking.

Others, however, have drawn a quite different conclusion from the available texts. We are told that there was a familiar and clear-cut distinction drawn in antiquity between the physical possession and the ownership of property, long before the general term for a right was introduced.[1] Ulpian

1. See David Daube, "Fashions and Idiosyncracies in the Exposition of the Roman Law of Property," in *Theories of Property*, ed. A. Paul and T. Flanagan (Waterloo, Canada: Wilfred Laurier University Press, 1979), p. 36.

uses the expression "one's own," which we would understand to mean that to which one has a right. Going beyond
property rights to what we would think of as political rights,
Demosthenes remarked, in connection with the issue of King
Philip's sovereignty over a Greek city, that "it is possible to
have what is another's," for "not all who have something
have what is their own."[2] And, as for moral rights, there is
the dictum discussed by Plato that justice is giving persons
their due, a dictum that seems to invoke some idea of rights.
But this is taken by Plato, perversely it might appear to modern readers, to mean only the idea involved in the siege men-
tality of a tribe or group surrounded by enemies,—as in the
thinking of the sentry who issues the challenge "Who goes
there, friend or foe?"—that what is due is the help to be
given friends—the members of one's own group—and the
harm to be given enemies—the hostile outsiders. This may
well strike the modern reader as symptomatic of Plato's undue readiness to divert attention away from what must have
been evident to his own contemporaries, namely, the relations between persons and what each owes to others, and
toward that inner condition of the soul whose "parts" are
functioning in that harmony with one another that he takes
to be constitutive of the "real" or "true" nature of justice.
Plato thereby creates the gap he fails to recognize between
this inner harmony and the consistent performance of such
just acts as the payment of one's debts, the telling of the
truth, and the keeping of one's word, during the course of
our dealings with one another.[3]

Are we to say, therefore, that the ancients did have the
idea of a right, lacking only a word for it? David Daube,
for one, minimizes the importance of the use of a general

2. See Daube, "Fashions," pp. 44–46, and Gregory Vlastos, "The Theory of
Social Justice in the Polis in Plato's *Republic*," in *Interpretations of Plato*, ed. H.
North (Leiden: Lugduni Batavorum, E. J. Brill, 1977), pp. 4–5.
3. See in this connection David Sachs, "A Fallacy in Plato's *Republic*," *Philosophical Review* 73 (1964): 141–159.

term to designate a right, declaring that "a social phenomenon no less than one in nature may considerably antedate
its labelling by a noun."[4] He goes on to cite the case of table
manners: some people at least did have a general idea of
good table manners long before the word "etiquette" came
into general use. Nevertheless, some cautions and comments
are in order lest we conclude, with undue haste, it seems to
me, that we may say quite unproblematically, that some notion of a moral right was, if only implicitly, familiar in antiquity.

1. Our talk about what is due or owed to others may suggest that, as in the case of our talk about what is one's own,
an idea of a right is involved. For when I do owe something
to someone, one can express the matter by saying that I am
indebted to that person, suggesting thereby the root idea of
a debt, something to the payment of which the person has
a right. But is this really true; is it true that whenever I owe
something to someone, the latter has a right against me?

Consider various cases in which favors or benefits of different sorts are received by me. Someone does me a favor,
for example, he drives me to the airport, and I ask him to
do this favor, saying, "I'll make it up to you." It would be
quite natural to construe what I say as a promise that the
person can count on me to return a favor of like importance
whenever the need arises. And it is true that often when
favors are bestowed on others, a promise, implicit or explicit, is involved. In cases of this sort, it seems clear enough
that a right is involved, that one's bluntly refusing to help
without offering a good excuse—thereby asking for a waiver
of the right—is much more than a case of ingratitude; it is
a case of refusing to acknowledge a right the person has
against one. But there are other cases to which the issue of
gratitude but not that of a right is pertinent: I am indebted

4. "Fashions."

to someone who has played an important role in my career
as a teacher, lawyer, or scientist, and it would be gross ingratitude on my part not to go to unusual lengths—in contrast with the case of a mere acquaintance to whom, as one
might put it, one is not indebted in any way—in helping the
person to who I am indeed very much obliged. Would it be
correct in such cases to say that I have violated his or her
right if I fail to show proper gratitude in the matter? Or, to
consider another case, the motor of the car I am driving
stalls, I move to the side of the road, and someone seeing
me in trouble stops his car and offers to help; without undue
effort he gets my car started again. He says, when I thank
him, "It was really nothing at all." He proceeds and, following him, I see his tire go flat so that he pulls off the road.
Do I violate his right when I ignore his plight by driving on
without offering him my help? Or do I show, by my failure
to stop and help, that I am an ungrateful wretch? Surely,
no right of his is involved; it is enough to remark on my
insensitivity to his plight and my ingratitude in order to
characterize my moral failure.

Indeed, and for what it is worth, when we speak of our
owing someone such and such, we make use of a word a
now obsolete usage of which conveys nothing more than the
idea of what ought to be done, as in Chaucer's line "You
owen to incline and bow your heart."[5] And when Hume
remarks about animals,—to whom, he argues, the rules of
justice do not apply—that we are indeed "bound, by the
laws of humanity, to give gentle usage to those creatures,"[6]
he might well have made his point by saying that this gentle
usage is something that, by the laws of humanity, we owe
animals.

The moral of all this is that the fact that something is due

5. See *Webster's: International Dictionary of the English Language* (1919), p.
1540.
6. *An Enquiry Concerning the Principles of Morals*, Sec. III.

or owed to others in itself does not establish that any right is involved.

2. Is the case of the introduction of a word for a right comparable, as Daube claims it is, to the case in which the word "etiquette" was introduced in order to designate already established good manners, the social phenomenon that existed before the introduction of this new word? Certainly, a physical phenomenon, for instance, the rate of increase in the fall of a body, existed long before the word "acceleration" was introduced in order to provide a more concise description of the motion of falling objects. But even here the introduction of the new word focuses attention upon an important recurrent phenomenon of moving objects. And certainly the manners that were acceptable in high social circles existed long before the word "etiquette" was introduced. But just as the introduction of the word "acceleration" served the purpose of providing an explanation of moving bodies by focusing attention upon a feature of this motion, so the introduction of the word "etiquette," which was to be used by all users of the language in and out of high court circles, by paupers and princes, served to point to and to promote new and presumably better standards of social behavior. It is a mistake to think that the introduction of a new word generally, let alone always, is a trivial matter.

We need to look more closely at the use of locutions like "one's own." "what is owed to someone," "one's due," etc., locutions that often involve some sort of notion of a moral right in their modern uses, in order to see what may or may not have been involved in their use in antiquity. But first we need to inquire into some distinctive features of rights, and for this purpose I shall begin with accounts of rights since first mention was made of them in early modern times.

2. Modern Conceptions of Rights

All of the foregoing leaves untouched the fact that the ancients did use certain locutions in order to convey what we should now recognize as rights. For they did, after all, distinguish between the physical possession of something and the having of it as one's own—political territory in the case of the sovereign and property in the case of citizens. And the latter, unlike slaves, could participate in various ways in the governance of their city states; there were, as we should now say, the rights that went with the responsibilities of citizenship in the Greek city state.

But consider what is said to be the first recorded use of a word for a right: William of Occam's defining of "natural right" as "a power of conform to right reason without an agreement or pact,"[1] presumably in contrast with a right established by means of a covenant or pact. However much the *de facto* power of individuals, as in the case of an armed robber, may have been conflated with the *de jure* power or authority, say, of a judge who may compel a person to hand over his money in payment of a fine imposed for some infraction of the law,[2] it is, I believe, safe to say that what

---

1. I. Berlin, in "Two Concepts of Liberty," *Four Essays on Liberty, (London and New York: Oxford University Press, 1969),* who refers in this connection to Michel Villey's discussion of the topic in *Leçon d'histoire de la philosophie du droit.* In addition, see Martin P. Golding's "The Concept of Rights: A Historical Sketch," in *Bioethics and Human Rights,* ed. E. Bandman and B. Bandman (Boston: Little, Brown, 1978), pp. 44–50.

2. H. L. A. Hart criticizes Hobbes for confusing these quite different notions, in his "Are There Any Natural Rights?," *The Philosophical Review* 64 (1955): 175–191.

Occam meant by "power" is authority. In any case, here we have new ideas brought together by the newly introduced word "right" in a manner that reflects an early indication of a kind of moral thinking that stands in sharp contrast with that which prevailed in antiquity. For whatever Occam and those who followed may have meant by "right reason," three aspects of their thought are clear. First, it is not only a select group who are now deemed to have rights, but anyone who is rational and capable therefore of ascertaining what the requirements of right reason are. Second, autonomy is ascribed to individuals insofar as they are capable, out of their own resources as rational beings, not merely of conforming to the requirements of the laws, human or divine, to which they are subject—for that can be done without any understanding of the laws' rationale—but of understanding how and why they are to order their own lives. Third, what now comes to the fore is the recognition of the importance of the freedom of individuals from undue constraints imposed by others, especially by the sovereign and those who serve him. It is this sense of the importance of the freedom of the individual that is brought into sharp focus in Blackstone's definition of a right as "a power to act as one thinks fit, without any restraint or control unless by the law of nature."[3]

In addition to these general comments on the moral thinking involved in the conception of rights that appears to be new in the early modern period, there are other matters to which attention needs to be directed. Here I shall consider in some detail the historically very important views of Locke not only in order to remove widespread misconceptions that have persisted even to this day but also in order to prepare the way for a discussion of the significance of the changes that have occurred in our thinking about rights.

3. See Golding, "The Concept of Rights," p. 48.

I

It is often said that Locke thinks of rights as liberties, in the sense that they are freedoms to act in certain ways with respect to which others are only bound or under an obligation not to interfere. Such a liberty (or privilege) is the right to walk on a sidewalk, drink a cup of tea in the privacy of one's home, and so on. Now Locke is often concerned as a great spokesman for liberties of individuals—one of his natural rights is indeed the very right to freedom—to emphasize the privileges individuals have not only in the state of nature but in civil society as well. But the supposition that, in the event of the threatened or actual violation of the natural rights of anyone, no one else is under any obligation to come to the assistance of the victim, is expressly denied by Locke.

> Everyone, as he is bound to preserve himself, and not to quit his station wilfully, so by the like reason, when his own preservation comes not in competition, ought he, as much as he can, to preserve the rest of mankind, and may not, unless it be to do justice on an offender, take away, or impair the life, or what tends to the preservation of the life, the liberty, health, limb, or goods of another.[4]

In the next paragraph he goes on further to declare:

> And that all men may be restrained from invading others' rights, and from doing hurt to one another, and the law of nature be observed, which willeth the peace and preservation of all mankind, the execution of the law of nature is, in that state, put into every man's hands, whereby everyone has a right to punish the transgressors of that law to such a degree, as may hinder its violation: For the law of nature would, as all other laws that concern men in this world, be in vain, if there were nobody that in the state of nature had a power to execute that law, and thereby preserve the innocent and restrain offenders. And if anyone in the state of nature may punish another for any evil he has done, everyone may do so.

4. *Second Treatise of Government*, para. 6.

As I have argued elsewhere[5] it should be quite clear that, according to Locke, men in the state of nature are under an obligation to others not merely to refrain from interference but as much as they can to preserve the life, liberty, and property to which others have a natural right. In civil society, which, according to Locke, has as the sole end of the transfer of the power of individuals to the government the preservation of the members of society "in their lives, liberties, and possessions," persons do not cease to have their rights. Nor do they cease to have any power, that is, authority, to demand their rights and to take such action as may be required—including the overthrow of the civil government itself—for the preservation of their lives, liberties, and possessions. And since they do not cease to have any of their natural rights, they do not cease to have whatever power or authority those rights confer upon them to seek redress from governmental tyranny.

What must be noted here is that Locke nowhere says, nor would it have made any sense for him to say, that in moving from the state of nature to that of civil society, men divest themselves of *all* authority they have in the state of nature, and with it any of the natural rights they have in that state.[6] Nor does he even suggest, when he declares that men are justified in doing what is within their power to come to the

---

5. In *Rights and Persons* (Berkeley, Los Angeles, London: University of California Press, 1977), p. 239.

6. Locke does declare that there are certain powers man gives up in subjecting himself to civil authority. He gives up that power he had in the state of nature to do whatever he sees fit, for the preservation of his life, since this "power" is "*to be regulated by the laws made by society*" (*Second Treatise*, para. 129, italics mine): And, as he says later (para. 131), the power, i.e., authority, men had in the state of nature in respect of their lives, liberties, and possessions is "to be so far disposed of by the legislative, as the good of the society shall require," this common good being the end of civil government. This authority "can never be supposed to extend farther, than the common good; but is obliged to secure everyone's property [liberty, life, and possessions], by providing against those . . . defects . . . that made the state of nature so unsafe and uneasy." Clearly there are limits to the transfer of "power" that occur when men subject themselves to "civil power." It is only "the power of punishing [that men] wholly give up" (para. 130).

aid of those whose lives, liberties, and possessions are threatened, that in appealing as he does to the law of nature, he
is appealing to a consideration that *competes* with and hence
may override the rights men have in common. For that law
of nature, which reason is capable of recognizing, is nothing
other than the moral requirement that follows from, and is
not competitive with, the natural rights of all men. In short,
it would have been absurd and inconsistent with Locke's
own views for him to think that the right of my neighbor
to his life, liberty, and possessions imposes no requirement
upon me to call for help when I see an armed intruder breaking into the house in which he lies fast asleep.[7]

Indeed, it would have been a glaringly obvious redun-
dancy, on the supposition that Locke's natural rights are
liberties, for him to have added the right to liberty to the
list of other natural rights.

II

The foregoing should suffice to show that Locke does not
think of individuals as egoistic. They are concerned to preserve their own lives and promote their own happiness—it
would be imprudent for them not to do so—but they are
not indifferent to one another's well-being. It is sometimes
said that Locke had an atomistic view of individuals; but if
this means that individuals were thought by Locke to be
without moral concern for one another, this is surely mistaken. For both in the state of nature and in civil society
men are required to act in behalf of one another, to punish
offenders against anyone in the former condition and to assist those whose lives, liberties, and possessions are threatened in civil society.

Locke indeed cites with approval the words of "the ju-

7. For a fuller discussion of these matters see the discussion on pp. 237–242
of my *Rights and Persons.*

dicious Hooker" that even in the state of nature "we are naturally induced to seek communion and fellowship with others"[8] and that "my desire . . . to be loved of [by] my equals in nature, as much as possible . . ., imposeth upon me a natural duty fo bearing to them . . . fully like affection."[9] And Locke himself remarks that in that same state of nature "each transgression [against others] may be punished to that degree, and with so much severity, as will . . . give him cause to repent."[10] The repentance is not merely suffering, but the suffering that is involved in the appreciation of the offense he has perpetrated, and with it, the remorse the penitent feels. Moreover, forgiving the offender, as indeed one should if he does repent, surely would not be possible unless the victim cared about him and was concerned to see him redeemed.

What has given some the notion that Locke's talk about rights involves an egoistic conception of individuals? Two considerations seem to me to be relevant here. First, talk about rights occurs—usually, at least—when persons stand on or demand their rights. Besides, all too often in the past such demands have been made by the economically and socially advantaged against those who seek to redress the balance of social injustice they have endured. Consider in this connection the extent to which appeals to rights have been made in the late nineteenth and early twentieth centuries in order to continue the practice of child labor, to suppress labor organizations, etc. It is understandable that such self-serving privilege-preserving appeals to rights have created the impression that talk about rights is closely tied to an egoistic conception of human beings.

Second, Locke held the view, shared by many individualists who followed him, that the world in which we live

8. *Second Treatise*, para. 15.
9. *Second Treatise*, para. 5.
10. *Second Treatise*, para. 12.

is a kind of America, seen through rosy seventeenth-century
glasses, in which men are capable, with relative self-suffi-
ciency, of carving out for themselves, from all that God has
given to all men in common, whatever it is they need for
the achievement of the goods that make life worthwhile.
Bound up with this unrealistic view is the idea that men have
only themselves to blame, because of their indolence, im-
prudence, or other character defects, if they fail to secure
these goods for themselves. We now know all too well that
poverty is not symptomatic of moral disease, that those who
are economically disadvantaged, far more often than not,
suffer through no fault of their own and only because of
social injustice. But it is with a view to *correcting* such injustice, rather than to perpetuating it, that we have in recent
years changed so markedly in our thinking about rights. For
the appeal to rights is now often made in order to redress
the injustices persons suffer—and in behalf of those persons.

3. Rights—Pro and Con

It was only a relatively short time ago that a philosopher could say confidently that "if we have a satisfactory theory about what we *ought to do*, we cannot have omitted anything of practical importance, that is, anything we have to know in order to know what we ought to do."[1] From this it might appear that we can safely ignore the topic of rights. Others, joining the chorus of those denigrating the importance of rights, declared that a right is only the reverse side of an obligation and can therefore be ignored in any philosophical discussion of what one ought to do.[2] Today talk about rights is commonplace in the philosophical literature. Someone unfamiliar with the literature might suppose that this change has occurred because of the recognition that there is a distinction to be made between being under an obligation *to someone* and being morally bound or obliged *to do*—the former serving as the ground of the latter—in consequence of which it is not a case of stuttering to say that one ought to do something because one is under an obligation to the person in question.[3] This, however, is not the reason.

The change, I believe, is due to the fact that even those

1. R. B. Brandt, *Ethical Theory* (Englewood Cliffs, N.J.: Prentice-Hall, 1959), p. 433.
2. For some other quotations from writers of the recent past who held such now archaic views, see Marcus G. Singer, "Recent Trends and Future Prospects in Ethics," *Metaphilosophy* 12 (1981): 217–218.
3. For a more detailed discussion of these matters, see my *Rights and Conduct* (Oxford: Blackwell, 1959), pp. 9–15.

who denigrate the philosophical importance of rights have come, belatedly of course, to appreciate their practical importance in human affairs through the various movements that have sought to remove social injustices and to ensure that nothing like the horrors of Nazism will ever be repeated. For the talk these days, in the public press as well as in the philosophical literature, is not only about rights construed as the moral property of moral agents but about "rights" that can hardly, if at all, be ascribed to moral agents: the alleged rights of all sentient creatures, fetuses and even newly fertilized ova, indeed, even the environment, including mountain streams. In short, it is not because rights have come to be recognized as grounds for the right and hence as not reducible to the latter that there is much talk these days in philosophical circles about moral rights but because of the widespread and increasingly effective appeals to rights that have been made to correct a wide variety of evils.

Those who rejected utilitarianism because that view seemed unable to provide any room for rights are now seeing utilitarians scramble to invoke them in claims of almost every sort concerning what we ought to do or to refrain from doing. This is ironical, for long before the present generation of utilitarians, turning their attention to various practical issues, found this new enthusiasm for rights, Mill had recognized their relevance to and importance for the concept of justice. During the course of his discussion of justice in the fifth chapter of *Utilitarianism*, Mill displayed a sensitivity to certain features of moral rights altogether unmatched by more recent utilitarians. I turn, therefore, to an exposition and discussion of Mill's account of certain moral rights in order to bring into sharper focus some features of these rights as we now do or should think of them.

4. Mill on Rights

I

Let me begin with an exposition of the main points of Mill's account, for it is by no means transparently clear.

Following an earlier tradition, Mill distinguishes between duties of perfect and duties of imperfect obligation. The former "are those duties in virtue of which a correlative *right* resides in some person or persons," whereas the latter, duties of imperfect obligations, "are those moral obligations which do not give birth to any right."[1] In duties of imperfect obligation, the obligations are "those in which, though the act is obligatory, the particular occasions of performing it are left to our choice, as in the case of charity and benevolence, which we are indeed bound to perform, but not toward any particular person, nor at any prescribed time." In duties of perfect obligation, such as the telling of the truth and the keeping of promises, with one possible sort of exception that I shall discuss later, there is no such discretionary power of the agent to decide when and where and to whom the obligatory act is to be performed.

Mill declares, "this distinction exactly coincides with that which exists between justice and the other obligations of morality." Accordingly, "[j]ustice implies something which it is not only right to do, and wrong not to do, but which some individual person can claim from us as his moral

1. All quotations and references, unless otherwise noted, are from and to, respectively, *Utilitarianism*, Chap. V. All italics are Mill's.

right," whereas "[n]o one has a moral right to our generosity or beneficence because we are not morally bound to practice those virtues toward any given individual." Indeed, "if a moralist attempts, as some have done, to make out that mankind generally, though not any given individual, have a right to all the good we can do them, he at once, by that thesis, includes generosity and beneficence within the category of justice" and "is obliged to say that our utmost exertions are *due* to our fellow creatures, thus assimilating them to debt." For where the issue of a right is involved, "[d]uty is a thing which may be *exacted* from a person, as one exacts a debt." Last, in acting justly, that is, in honoring someone's right, one provides the right holder with some good; in acting unjustly one deprives the right holder of some good or visits some evil upon that person.

Later I shall discuss certain of these claims; they are, I believe, mistaken. But for the present I list a number of Mill's observations that demonstrate his characteristic willingness to make concessions to common sense views. In most cases, they also demonstrate a sensitivity to moral matters unmatched by latter-day utilitarians.

First, Mill recognizes and approves of the view of thinkers in his day, a view also held by many at least in our own, that "a person is understood to deserve good if he does right, evil if he does wrong." Here, clearly, the thought that deserving good and deserving evil cannot be identified with the idea that the good and evil will encourage and deter, respectively, right and wrong conduct. How this view, widespread even in our day, can even *seem* to be justified on utilitarian grounds, rather than on the basis of some such obscure idea as the requirement of cosmic justice or the restoration of the balance of good and evil, it is difficult to understand. As for Mill's endorsement of the precept "of returning good for evil" and of showing mercy, however much utility may be promoted by such acts, it is surely the fact that such conduct is, as such, virtuous that comes most readily to mind as the ground for approval.

Second, unlike act utilitarians, who are sometimes prepared to regard the special treatment given to the members of one's own family or close friends at best as well-meaning provincialism, Mill declares that "A person would be more likely to be blamed than applauded for giving his family or friends no superiority in good offices over strangers when he could do so without violating any other duty." For such persons have special rights, and if preference is given to them, this is no violation of the requirement of impartiality. For impartiality, where rights are concerned, while "an obligation of justice, may be said to mean exclusively influenced by the considerations which it is supposed ought to influence the particular case in hand." So it is with the equality that we are indeed required to observe in our treatment of others. It would be moral blindness to treat all cases alike, without regard to the special rights of and obligations to those close to us, just as it would be to subscribe to the doctrine of equal protection to the rights of all while, in the case of slave countries, supporting "the most outrageous inequality in the rights themselves." The requirements of impartiality and inequality do not imply either that woolly minded and generalized love for others that is oblivious to the special rights of close friends, parents, children, and siblings or any indifference to the rights of those who are enslaved or oppressed.

Third, "it is confessedly unjust to *break faith* with anyone: to violate an engagement, either express or implied, or disappoint expectations raised by our own conduct, at least if we have raised those expectations knowingly or voluntarily." In saying this Mill must surely have meant that in addition to cases in which a promise has been given to others, there are the mutual understandings created or maintained by our words and deeds which are enough to create or to foster, respectively, the rights of others. To declare that one did not promise, when one deliberately "raised expectations" by one's words or deeds, is nothing less than transparent Pharisaism.

Fourth, Mill is surely correct in declaring that anyone who violates the right of a person "ought to be punished in some way or other . . . if not by law, by the opinion of his fellow creatures; if not by opinion, by the reproaches of his own conscience."

Finally, there is the point that in the case of an injustice there is, as Mill puts it, "some assignable person who is wronged." For it is *this* particular person, the right holder, whom I wrong when, for example, I break faith with him, *that* particular person whom I wrong when I fail to give the individual in question the special consideration I ought to give a close friend, a parent, or a child.

This last point seems obvious enough, hardly worth mentioning; but it is important, for, like the previous ones, it does provide a good test of the correctness of Mill's analysis of justice and the rights it involves. Does Mill's analysis provide a satisfactory basis for the several considerations I have enumerated, considerations of which Mill, unlike other utilitarians, was sensible and in respect of which Mill deserves the credit he has not always received? In exploring this question I shall have occasion to comment on certain features of moral rights as we now do or should think of them.

II

Mill begins his positive account of justice by specifying two factors involved in what he calls "the sentiment of justice," both of which he says are natural and either are or resemble instincts. The first is the impulse to repel or harm those who harm us, in respect of which human beings are like animals. The second is our common interest in repressing actions that harm mankind, an interest we have by virtue of (a) the intelligence that enables us to see that certain kinds of action are socially harmful, and (b) the sympathy we have for those who suffer. The resentment against someone who harms us—which in itself, that is, insofar as it is a mere feeling, "has nothing moral in it"—is moralized, that is to say, is a case of moral resentment, only because we have a common interest in preventing persons from engaging in socially pernicious forms of conduct. We may at first resent having been harmed by someone simply because *we* have suffered harm; but if we go on to consider the fact that the kind of action that harmed us is socially pernicious, the resentment we feel, because of our sympathy with a society that would suffer from that kind of action, is now moral resentment. As Mill puts it, "just persons [resent] a hurt to society, though not otherwise a hurt to themselves, and [do not resent] a hurt to themselves, however painful, unless it be of the kind society has a common interest with them in the repression of."

And as he goes on,

> [i]t is no objection against this doctrine to say that, when we feel our sentiment of justice outraged, we are not thinking of society at large or of any collective interest, but only of the individual case. It is common enough, certainly, though the reverse of commendable, to feel resentment merely because we have suffered pain; but a person whose resentment is really a moral feeling . . . though he may not say expressly to himself that he is standing up for the interest of society, certainly does feel that he is asserting a rule which is for the benefit of others as well as for his own. If he is not feeling this, if he is regarding the act solely as it affects him individually, he is not consciously just; he is not concerning himself about the justice of his actions.[2]

2. The importance of following the rule in Mill's thinking is brought home by his remarks about Kant: "When Kant . . . propounds as the fundamental principle of morals, 'So act that thy rule of conduct might be adopted as a law by all rational beings,' he virtually acknowledges that the interest of mankind collectively . . . must be in the mind of the agent when conscientiously deciding on the morality of the act. Otherwise he uses words without a meaning. . . . To give any meaning to Kant's principle, the sense put upon it must be that we ought to shape our conduct

What sort of rule must he "feel that he is asserting"? A rule that states a "duty of perfect obligation," compliance with which is essential for the existence of human life in any form in which it is worthwhile. What is meant then by my having a right? "To have a right . . . is, I conceive, to have something which society ought to defend me in the possession of." And why ought it to do so? The reason for Mill is its extraordinary utility, the benefit to all of us of compliance with the rule. Notice, however, that it is not mere conformity but compliance with the rule—submission to it, as it were—that is called for, if the feelings we have that an act is just or unjust are feelings of moral commendation when the act honors the right, moral condemnation when the act violates the right.

III

I turn now to an examination of some of the features of Mill's account I described above in Section I. Later I will determine whether Mill's positive analysis of rights can provide room for some of the other considerations that are in fact testimony to his good moral sense.

1. Consider the traditional distinction endorsed by Mill between duties of perfect obligation and duties of imperfect obligation, the former being those that, as the medievals put it, can be commanded, the latter those that can only be

---

by a rule which all rational beings might adopt *with benefit to their collective interest.*" But this insistence upon the theoretical role of rules in morals does not comport well with his remarks in *Utilitarianism*, Chap. II, about the practical importance of the moral rules he calls "secondary principles." He compares these with the nautical tables upon which the mariner is obliged to rely because of the practical, not theoretical, impossibility of calculating his position on the ocean by using observational data together with the principles of astronomy. So, too, with his statement that we are to appeal directly to the principle of utility in the event of a conflict of rules—for if direct appeal may be made in this case, why not in the justification of any single act if sufficient knowledge is available?

counseled.[3] Much of the talk by utilitarians about the great utility of the practice of promising, in contrast with that of giving charity or displaying generosity, is inspired by the view, advanced by Hume and often repeated today, that a promise involves a mutually beneficial exchange of benefits and burdens, an eminently useful quid pro quo arrangement between promisor and promisee.

Hume was sensible enough to recognize that such an arrangement between those who are close to each other would often cheapen the relation, and on this ground denied that promises are entered into by those close to each other. But this, surely, is going too far. I come home in the evening after an unusually exhausting day at the office, but my wife wants very much to have me go with her to the movies after dinner. Would it be odd or unseemly if I promise to do so the next night, so that I might recover from my exhaustion? And does every case of a promise I make to my wife involve an exchange of benefits? If I see her yearning for a dress displayed in the shop window, do I assure her that I'll buy it for her when I receive my next paycheck so that she will continue to maintain the house or serve as a compliant bed-partner? Why indeed should I adjust my own affairs and stand ready at the appointed time to keep my word? Because I will be condemned if I do not? This would hardly be an admirable reason, even if it did occur to me. Because it will erode public confidence that promises will be kept? To this J. D. Mabbott's well-known rejoinder to Hume is surely decisive: "Keep it quiet."[4] Nor will a feeling of sympathy as diffuse as it is general, a feeling directed at anyone, past, present, or future, known or unknown, whose interests may be thought to be affected by the manner in which we conduct ourselves with respect to "the rule of promises," suffice

---

3. Again, all quotations and references, unless otherwise noted, are from and to, respectively, *Utilitarianism*, Chap. V.
4. In "Punishment," *Mind* 48 (1939): 152–167.

to explain "the sentiment of morality." One contributes to a fund to help those starving in Africa or one goes to the aid of someone injured on the street, not because of some general feeling of sympathy but because one cares for those who need our help. And in the case in which a perfect stranger promises to return something of value if he is allowed to borrow it, one does not, if one is at all sensible, accept the promise because of one's belief that the stranger, being endowed with this general sympathy, will for that reason keep his word. In cases in which one is given a promise by some stranger to do such and such for thus and so, one does not normally accept the promise without, as it were, "sizing him up" with a view to forming some reasonable estimate of the person's character—that he cares enough about others that he will not let them down. For in paradigm cases in which promises are given and accepted, cases in which, as it were, the promises go through, the persons involved care about each other. Caring, however, is something that goes much more deeply in our lives than the having of some general and passing feeling of sympathy that usually occurs in the course of our relations with casual acquaintances or total strangers. I shall have more to say about the difference between being sympathetic and caring in chapter 8.

Whatever may be true of the administration of justice, especially in the lower courts, in which usually, as it is familiarly expressed, the law is the law, in normal moral contexts the rational concern with the rights of others and the willingness to assume those obligations that go with them cannot be understood independently of the concern with the well-being of others. The distinction between "duties of perfect obligation" and "duties of imperfect obligation" in which the former are received as commandments that must be followed without any considerations of our feelings in the matter—"Duty, stern voice of necessity"[5]—will not do.

5. Friedrich Schiller, *On the Aesthetic Education of Man*, trans. Elisabeth M.

This of course is to reject the traditional doctrine of Natural Law, in which this distinction was employed, and with it the views of Kant, for whom the Law Giver is replaced by Sovereign Reason, and of neo-Kantians like Prichard, who distinguish sharply between considerations of duty and virtue. It simply makes no sense to talk about the obligations correlative with moral rights as if these were quite intelligible independently of the requirements of benevolence or, as Hume put it, "the softer virtues." I shall say more about this below, in chapter 8.

2. The distinction between these so-called duties involves, in Mill's account of them, the thought that in the cases in which rights are concerned it is not a matter of choice for those who are obliged—as it is in the case of "duties of imperfect obligation," such as those of benevolence and charity—when and to whom they ought to meet their obligations. It would appear, then, that it is not up to parents or promisors to decide when, where, and how they are to meet their respective obligations.

(i) Consider the case of the obligation of parents to provide the care, training, and moral education required for the proper development of their children into adulthood. Although their obligations to their offspring are to those particular individuals, it is obvious to anyone who is or has been a parent that *what* they are to do on any particular occasion must be left for parental decision based upon their good sense of the particular circumstances of the case, their own means, the stage of the development of their offspring, the latter's character and temperament, and the specific interests their offspring does or should have, and *when* and *where* they are to do it, unhesitatingly and as a matter of course. Those who have been sensitive and conscientious

---

Wildinson and L. A. Willoughby (Oxford: Clarendon Press, Oxford, 1967), p. 217. See also "Stern daughter of the voice of God," in Wordsworth's "Ode to Duty."

parents, who have watched their children develop from infancy, and who change in the ways in which they deal with
their children as they progress toward adulthood can appreciate how difficult it can be to meet their obligations to
their offspring. And this, surely, is altogether unlike a duty
that, as Mill puts it, "may be exacted from a person as one
exacts a debt."

(ii) Consider a promise—a central case, one made seriously, not frivolously, on a matter of importance and in
which responsible persons are involved. Since the obligation
created is a "duty of perfect obligation," it is not up to the
agent, on Mill's view, to decide on what particular occasion,
as in the case of benevolence, to perform the morally required act. On Mill's view, the promisee is in a position of
authority to demand the payment of the moral debt in the
same way as a creditor who is in possession of a demand
note. Mill recognizes that obligations, along with their correlative rights, may conflict, in which case we are to appeal
to the underlying principle of utility in order to adjudicate
the competing claims; but this is not a discretionary authority of the morally indebted agent. It is, rather, a matter
of moral necessity, for in the absence of such an appeal to
the first principle, there can only be moral impotence and
disaster. In normal cases in which no such conflicts of secondary principles occur, it is the moral creditor—the promisee—who stands in a position of authority, to press his
demand for payment of the moral debt that was incurred
in the making of the promise.

Will this do? I want to show that it involves much too
narrow a view of the authority of both of the persons involved in the promise transaction and of the moral burdens
assumed. For there is not only the authority created by the
promise, but the authority of both promisor and promisee
as moral agents who *as such* are concerned with the well-
being of others.

First, I promise someone something he needs in order to

pursue some specific interest; but by the time I am to make good on my promise, he no longer has that interest. Suppose there is no competing obligation. Surely it would be unreasonable for the person to demand that I keep my word. Indeed, we think that he ought to release me from my obligation—to relinquish his right—if the keeping of my promise is likely to cause me any inconvenience. But if he is unable to do so—I am away and out of reach—the fact that the promise cannot be relegated to the dead past is shown by the fact that, when I finally realize that he no longer has any interest in the matter and decide not to keep my word, I owe him an explanation in order to ensure that good moral relations with him have not been jeopardized.

Second, I promise someone a widget—something especially useful for small weeding jobs in his garden, but not indispensable, since he could use a narrow trowel. But unexpectedly, I cannot, without considerable difficulty, get the widget to him in time for him to use it. I have promised, he has a right, and having weighed my burden against the small gain he could derive from the use of the implement, I decide not to keep my promise. Am I wrong? Surely I must weigh the quite particular circumstances of the case: how burdensome it would be for me to get the widget to him, how great his burden would be if I did not do so, how my moral relations have been with him in the past, his sense of my moral character, and certainly his character and temperament. Would he be touchy about my breaking my promise, or would he be unconcerned, confident that I must have had very good reason to do so? And suppose now that I had misjudged matters, or that because of the pressures upon me I had in fact acted in bad faith: how is he to react? Whatever authority promisees may have, in demanding their rights, in waiving them, or in relinquishing them, they have the burden of deciding how they are to deal with promisors who have transgressed against them. Here no general rule will supplant the good judgment needed to attend carefully to the circumstances in the case; this involves careful attention to the needs and interests of the other party, his temperament, his demeanor, past performances in similar situations, etc. These are burdens *he* must assume, corresponding to his authority as a right holder; and in assuming these burdens it is surely up to him to decide how he is to comport himself with the other party to the moral transaction.

Third, I make a promise to someone. He has a right against me; and, if we view the promise from the other direction, I am under an obligation to him. But I now see what neither of us could have foreseen when I promised, and what even now he is unable to see because of his special circumstances, namely, that if I keep my promise and he goes through with the plan that occasioned it, he and perhaps others would be harmed. Should I keep my promise? We can imagine cases of this kind in which there are no competing rights and in which promises ought to be broken. Why? Not because such promises become null and void—for even here explanations and justifications are called for, not because of the threatened harm but because of the rights and obligations created by the promises. For these rights and obligations are not canceled simply because of the harm that looms ahead. In cases of this sort, promisors have assumed not only the burdens of their obligations but also the authority—because of their underlying concern, as moral agents, with the well-being of those to whom they are obliged—not to meet their obligations, that is, to deny them their rights.

(iii) Consider, finally, the case in which a promisor wrongs a promisee. A promise has been made and, in failing to keep it, the promisor has committed a moral offense. Suppose too that it is no small matter; an important plan or project was at stake, the success of which was dependent upon the keeping of the promise. The victim may condemn the offender, and so should we if the matter had been of sufficient importance. But in certain circumstances forgiveness may be called for. The offender, realizing his guilt, suffers remorse—he suffers because he recognizes the moral injury he has caused—and he repents, showing by word and demeanor that he is determined not to repeat the offense. Surely forgiveness is in order; not to extend it is to pile one's offense upon that of another, and two wrongs have never made a right.

To forgive someone is not the same as to cease condemning that person, for one can do the latter in many different ways. It is, rather, to make clear in thought and word that one no longer holds the misdeed *against* an offender, that one is prepared to resume with trust and confidence normal moral relations with the offender. The guilt is no longer a factor in one's dealings with the perpetrator of the misdeed; it can be as cheerfully put out of one's mind as one puts an end to the moral suffering—the pangs of guilt—of the offender. Forgiveness relieves this sort of moral distress, unlike shame, which persists as long as the recollection of the shameful incident remains.

On this matter Locke thought that, as he put it, "he who has suffered the damage has a right to demand in his own name, and he alone can remit [it]."[6] Certainly it would be odd for me to forgive someone with whom I have only the slightest acquaintance, for trespassing against a third person, a total stranger. But it is not true, so it seems, that no one other than the victim can forgive an offender. Son about father, living or dead: "I could never forgive him for the abominable way in which he treated my mother." Notice "my mother" rather than "his wife," for here the son speaks *for* his mother—he puts himself in the place of or acts as a surrogate for his mother in judging the situation. This case is, however, parasitic upon the central sort of case in which

6. *Second Treatise*, para. 11.

one speaks, with the authority of the person trespassed against, for oneself.

There is, then, the authority of the one who has suffered moral injury to forgive and the requirement of the guilty to repent and, if possible, to make restitution.

In short, the analogy drawn between the obligation to keep a promise, this being only one example of a so called "duty of perfect obligation," and the obligation of someone who has signed a note payable on demand, will not do. Morally speaking, some demand notes should be torn up, but in courts of law they can be used to force payment whether or not it would be morally improper to do so.

3. I turn now to Mill's notion that the meeting of an obligation to someone, as in the case of the keeping of a promise, is a case of providing that person with a good.

There are, to begin with, deviant or degenerate usages of the verb "to promise." One promises oneself a bottle of wine for dinner; and a father promises his errant child a licking. These, clearly, are borrowed uses. In the former, one shores up one's resolution by the sotto voce employment of the verb, borrowing the heavy moral overtones that go with it, in what clearly is a matter devoid of any moral implications. In the latter circumstance a similar borrowing occurs: the use of the verb underscores to the child the father's determination to carry out the threat.

There are, however, promises involving two and three persons which need to be considered. Usually, when one person makes a promise to another to do (or to abstain from doing) something, there is some plan or project of the promisee to the success of which the promise-keeping act or abstention is thought to contribute (or some threatened intervention the promise is designed to forestall), and in these cases some good of the promisee is at issue. But there are cases, by no means rare, deviant, or eccentric, in which it is not the promisee that benefits from the keeping of the promise.

(i) Consider these examples. A wife who is worried about her husband's health gets him to promise that he will not follow his usual practice of eating junk food while working at his desk but take time off for a nutritious and leisurely meal. Again, a mother, worried about her son's propensity to ignore his studies and to waste his time and energies, gets him to promise that when away at college, he will diligently pursue his studies and not stay up all hours of the night in frivolous activities. Surely, it is the promisor in such cases, not the promisee, who stands to benefit.

It may be objected that the promisee does in fact benefit from having her fears, anxiety, and worry put to rest by the promise. No doubt some good is served by the promises made in the examples cited; there would be no point in obtaining the promises unless some good purposes were to be served. But the fears, anxiety, and worry are put to rest not by the *keeping* of the promises made but by the *making* of those promises; and what is at issue here is Mill's view that the meeting of the obligations in question is the conferring of some good upon the promisee. The point made against Mill's view is in no way weakened by the fact that these promises would not be solicited and made, had the promisees not reposed any trust in the promisors to meet their obligations. Further, if the promisees do benefit from the promise-keeping acts—the wife is pleased to see that her husband is not troubled by his usual indigestion—this benefit is derived from the benefit received by the promisors keeping of their promises. It would be implausible in the extreme to argue that in all such cases the promises are solicited with a view to serving this derivative benefit.

There is a further point that needs to be made about these sorts of cases—call them "first-person promises"—which also applies to cases of third-party promises, to which I shall turn next. And it is this point, as I shall show, that needs to be emphasized in order to see what is fundamentally wrong with Mill's accounts of rights. For we must ask ourselves what it is that is bad about the worry, the relief from which is the good that the promise provides the promisee. Does the worrying consist *simply* in having some unpleasant or undesirable feeling? And would it help matters to say that it is this unpleasant feeling together with the thought, in the case of the wife who worries about her husband's health, of her husband's wolfing his junk food while working at his desk? Surely it is not some sort of experience, some internal impression, over and above this thought that is unpleasant; it is this thought *itself* that is unpleasant. And if she did have this thought, would the thought be enough to establish the fact that she worried, if that thought were some passing thought she had one, two, or three times during the day but which in no way interfered with her usual activities and the satisfaction these gave her?

We need to understand, I believe, what a central case of worrying is, in which there is no concealment from others of the fact that we worry—for concealing one's worry is something we learn only after we learn what it is to worry, just as we learn what it is to lie after we learn what it is to tell the truth. So here we need to think of a full-blooded case of our wife's worry. The thought of her husband's eating habit at lunch weighs heavily on her during the day, so much so that she appears distracted. In reading a magazine she may follow the words on the page but not the sense, coming to, with a start, when she realizes that she has not understood what she has been reading. She hesitates when carrying out the most routine tasks, as if her mind is not on what she is doing. When she prepares a meal that is normally routine for her, she will absentmindedly leave out an essential ingredient. When she listens to music, her mind wanders to the unhappy thought of her husband's indigestion. When someone speaks to her and asks her a question she may well be inattentive and come to, with a start, when she realizes that she has not been listening. In these and in countless other ways she fails *as an agent* to do successfully the sorts of things over which she has acquired the normal mastery, and does as a matter of course.

Further, as a wife she is interested in her husband's well-being and engages in various activities in the course of her wifely conduct, in order to maintain it. And surely her husband's failure to have nourishing food at lunchtime, when the pressures of his work can be put aside, can only place in jeopardy the efforts she makes to promote or preserve her husband's health.

We must not think, therefore, that the worry and the concern, the relief from which the promise is designed to secure, is some internal feeling quite intelligible independently of the agency of the person who worries and is concerned enough to elicit the promise.

(ii) Consider H. L. A. Hart's example of a third-person promise: X promises Y, who is about to leave on an extended trip, to look after Y's aged mother, Z, during his absence.[7] In order to avoid the complications that arise when Z learns that X has promised and when X learns that Z has learned about the promise,[8] let us suppose that Z remains unaware of the promise. Here Y is the right holder and X is under an obligation to Y, but it is Z who is to be the beneficiary. Here, as in the examples discussed above, it will not do to defend Mill on the ground that Y will benefit by being relieved of any worry about the well-being of his mother. For *that* relief is provided by the promise X has made to Y, not by the keeping of the promise; and if Z benefits from the care X supplies her in Y's absence, it is not the right holder but a third party that receives the ben-

7. In his paper "Are There Any Natural Rights?"
8. For a discussion of some of these complications, see my *Rights and Persons*, pp. 51–52.

efit. And here, too, the comments made above on the nature of the worry that is alleviated by the making of the promise and on the interest and agency of the promisee are appropriate.

IV

I turn now to the last of the considerations listed in Section I of this chapter, in which, as I remarked, Mill demonstrates his sensitivity to some of the familiar features of rights. Here it will suffice for my purpose to discuss a matter that may seem to be too obvious to be worth mentioning, namely, that when a right has been violated, there is, as he puts it, "some assignable person who is wronged." If *A* breaks faith with someone who has a right against *A*, it is *that* particular person whom *A* wrongs. Can Mill accommodate this simple and quite obvious fact in his utilitarian theory of moral rights? I shall attempt to show now that he cannot, and that we must look elsewhere for a satisfactory understanding of what is involved in a moral right.

Consider, to begin with, a simple case in which *A* promises to help *B* in a project of some importance, and in which, because *A* fails to keep the promise, *B* suffers some material damage. The mere damaging of *B*, by itself, is not wronging *B*; for this could happen because of circumstances that were unforeseeable and over which neither *A* nor *B* had any control. *B* in that case might lash out at *A*, that is, retaliate in kind, but could not reasonably condemn *A* and claim that he had suffered moral injury at his hands. What makes any damage *B* suffers *moral* damage, that is, what makes an action of *A* a case of wronging *B*, according to Mill, is that the action is a breach of a rule the observance of which is especially useful for mankind. In breaching such a rule, *A*'s action is harmful not only to *B* but to everyone else. It is in this way, that is, in being socialized, according to Mill, that *A*'s action is moralized and therefore is a case of wronging *B*. And it is for this same reason that if *B* has a right, society ought to protect him in the possession of whatever it is to which he has that right.

Setting aside for the moment the fact that the utility of the rule, say the rule of promises, can be preserved by the secrecy of the rule-breaking act, there is the matter of understanding how it can be that what happens to the one who suffers the injury, namely *B*, can become more than mere injury but *moral* injury, that is, wronging, because of what happens to others, including the countless number of people completely unknown to either *A* or *B*. How can wronging *B* depend upon the fact that C, D, E, . . . , and so on indefinitely are injured? The reply will be, of course, that something like this occurs in the case of the wrongness of an action. For a given action may be wrong because of its consequences, and aren't the consequences entities other than the act itself?

But this will not do. To preserve the analogy one would have to say that the wrongness of this particular act depends upon the fact that other acts, similar in some relevant respect to this one, have similar effects, for example, in being injurious. And how it is that an injurious act becomes *morally* harmful, that is, a case of wronging a person, because each of the *other* acts like it are injurious in the same nonmoral respect? It seems paradoxical to say that a nonmorally injurious act becomes morally injurious simply because it is endlessly repeated. But Mill's response to this objection would be that it misses the point, that it is the breach of a highly useful *rule*, which in every case is injurious, that makes the nonmoral injury to *B* a case of wronging *B*. For the notion of having a right is understood by Mill in terms of the benefit to be received by following, in the given case as in every other, a rule that is eminently useful; and if one asks why one should follow the rule, there is nothing other than the principle of utility to which appeal can and need be made.

We should, therefore, consider not only cases in which, as Mabbott pointed out, utility may be preserved by rule-breaking acts that, being secret, in no way erode the general utility of the rule but also cases in which there is moral offense and in which the injury is to someone other than the morally injured person. I want to rest the case against Mill not on Mabbott's answer to Hume—good as that answer is and much as it applies to Mill as well—but on cases of promises in which the moral offense is clearly different from the injury suffered and in which it is equally clear that the person who suffers the injury is different from the person who is wronged. In the example previously given of a third-person promise—X promises Y to look after Z—suppose that Y's mother, Z, suffers because X neglects his obligation to Y. Then, however much Z (who remains ignorant of the promise) may complain that X failed to help her when he became aware of her plight, it is surely not Z but Y, discovering on his return that his mother has suffered from neglect, who has every reason to complain that X has let him down, betrayed him by breaking his promise. So it is in the case of the first-person promise of a husband to his wife, to have a good lunch rather than the usual junk food eaten hastily at his desk. The failure of the husband to keep his promise is a breach of his wife's trust, and she has good reason to complain that *she* has been let down—a matter, surely, that is different from any injury the husband may have done to himself.

It would be implausible in the extreme for Mill to attempt to meet the objection posed by these counterexamples by dismissing them as deviant, derivative, or questionable cases of promises, as were the examples of the so-called promises to have a bottle of wine for dinner or to punish a misbehaving child. The cases with which I am now concerned are quite unproblematic: their breachings constitute cases of moral injury to persons other than those who would have benefited from the promise-keeping acts. In each of them it is "an assignable person" other than one who has suffered an injury, an evil consisting of the deprivation of some good, who has been wronged.

In philosophy we can profit from the lessons of the mistakes of others. What then can we learn from Mill's failure on this point? Here it seems to me that the picture Mill gives us of the morally relevant features of personhood is impossible narrow—and not surprisingly so, given his commitment to utilitarianism. For on that doctrine what is quintessentially important is the fact that persons enjoy goods and suffer evils—pleasures and pains, or, as some would have it, the satisfaction and the frustration of desires—so that the moral qualities of persons and their conduct are assessable simply in terms of their tendency to promote the one and minimize the other. Hence it is that utilitarians view admirable character traits as admirable solely because of their consequences, and so too with any of the considerations that weigh on us in our moral judgments. Specifically in the case of justice and injustice the sole determinants of our moral appraisals are taken by them to be conformity with, or the breach of, rules of conduct eminently useful to mankind. In short, rights are defined by Mill in terms of considerations of this sort, and given this reductionism and the tunnel-visioned conception of moral agency, the result is inevitable. It becomes impossible to understand how it is that we judge as we do that there are the "assignable" persons who are wronged when we fail to meet our obligations to them, fail to give preferential treatment to our friends and the members of our families and, in general, break faith with others.

Consider Mill's declaration that if a person "is not feeling [that he is asserting a rule which is for the benefit of others as well as for his own], if he is regarding the act solely as it affects him individually . . . he is not concerning himself about the justice of his actions." Now this does smell fishy. For if someone breaks faith with me, violates some right I have against him, isn't there a moral issue involved simply because of the fact that *he* is under an obligation to *me*, that *I* have counted on *him* to meet that obligation and in doing so justify the trust *I* have reposed in *him*, whatever may be true of the social inutility of such breaches of faith? Indeed, wouldn't we even say of one who *thought* ill of a person because he had been misled into thinking that the latter had broken faith with him, that he had done him an injustice in *thinking* ill of him? The point is that these are moral relations in which we stand with others, relations in which we trust them, as they do us, to honor their obligations to us as we honor our obligations to them. And it is with the relations between *us*—not the indefinitely many others, known and unknown, past, present, and future—with whom, in our thoughts and deeds, we are concerned as moral beings.

To a utilitarian, the talk about moral relations between specific, "assignable" persons may seem mysterious, as if the model of such a relation were such a simple matter as Tom's being taller than John. But enough has been said to make clear what sort of relation we have. To say that A has a right against B is equivalent to saying that B has an obligation to A—a moral relation, the features of which we have been at pains to spell out in our discussion of the obligation of promises. It is not to say that B ought, or ought not, to do *x*, for it is no pleonasm to say that B ought, or ought not, to do *x because* of the obligation he has to A. Here the prepositional phrase "to A" marks the moral relation in question.

And we have spelled out the features of this moral relation in describing the authority and burdens of both of the persons standing in the moral relation. For, as we have seen, these have a crucial bearing on the kind of stance each must take toward the other, in thought no less than in action, and in ways that vary broadly with the unforeseen no less than the foreseen circumstances that may arise. This involves, in the thinking of both persons, a sense of the relevance of various considerations of the kind we have enumerated, considerations that serve to justify or to condemn conduct that affects the trust between them. And in the event that condemnation may appear to be in order, it involves a sense of the need for explanations, excuses, restitutions, or demonstrations of remorse, and for the forgiveness that terminates the moral ostracism of the offender. This implies that those who stand in this moral relation, the main features of which I have only very briefly indicated, are members of a moral community that involves the trust that is possible among its members and the understanding they share of the reasons for, or the considerations that can be adduced in support of, the measures taken in thought, word, or deed with respect to their conduct and character.

These are the features of the moral relation in which one person stands to another, a relation in which some right is involved. And notice that while I have not offered a formal definition of a right, I have sketched some of the main conceptual features of the sorts of rights we have been considering, features anyone receiving a proper moral education will come to appreciate. And, certainly, in seeing *this*, it is clear that I have rejected the reductionism of Mill's account, no less than that of other utilitarians, in which talk about rights and the obligations these entail are explicable simply in terms of right conduct.

Why ought one, for example, to keep a promise? Not because there is a rule compliance with which has been shown, by the experience of the human race, to be eminently useful, and the breaching of which has been proved eminently pernicious (that this is so not to the point, although it is worth remarking that no one has gathered the relevant empirical data). We should keep it because the so-called rule serves only to single out one very good but not necessary

compelling reason for acting in the appropriate way.[9] Someone who "questioned" the so-called rule of promises would
demonstrate thereby that he had not, or possibly could not,
understand what a promise is. One ought to do x, because
doing x is the meeting of an obligation to someone who has
received a promise from one. Why ought one to meet that
obligation? Here it is that justification comes to an end; only
an explanation of what is *meant* by saying that there is that
obligation, including all of its complex conceptual ramifications, will do.

Earlier I commented upon the import of the relief from
worry provided by the making of those first- and third-person promises to which I paid particular attention. I remarked that the nature of a worry that is dispelled by these
promises is such that it erodes the worrier's agency and that,
bad as it may be because of its unpleasantness, its badness
does not consist merely in the worrier's inner unpleasant
feeling. It consists rather in the manner in which it distracts
one—in thought or deed—from whatever business is at
hand in which interests are pursued and the goods that these
interests define are brought to pass. It is *this* sense of the
agency of the person, not the sense narrowly restricted to
the bringing to pass of good or bad experiences, that is cru-
cially important. And among the goods defined by our interests is that good defined by our common interest in the
moral community, to the preservation and promotion of
which all moral agents, regardless of their moral achievements or failures, are committed.

9. More on this last point in chap. 8, Sec. II, below.

5. Human or Fundamental Rights

It might seem odd, particularly to today's unsophisticated reader of Mill—a reader who has not acquired a philosophical ideology that obscures the importance and the variety of rights—that nowhere do we find in Mill's discussion any mention of natural or human rights. Let me begin my discussion of this topic with some preliminary remarks about the views of Locke, views that must be taken into account in any adequate discussion of natural or human rights.

Locke, it should be noted, did not include the rights created by promises in his list of natural rights, even though the right of a promisee plays an important role in the state of nature. For it is this right that is involved in the social contract, the terms of which call for the preservation of the natural rights of all subjects during the course of the sovereign's exercise of power. These natural rights are fundamental, therefore, not in the sense that they impose requirements that stand highest in the order of social utility, but in a quite different sense.

For Locke, natural rights stem from "the law of nature . . . and reason, which is that law";[1] for the law of nature, divinely based as it is, is not an arbitrary dictate of God's will but one founded on the rational nature of God and hence on reason itself. Locke appears to think of these natural rights, which are called for by the law of nature, as fundamental not only to those rights that men have in civil

1. *Second Treatise*, para. 6.

society but also to all other rights that exist even in the state of nature. Writing about the right that all men have in the state of nature to punish any offender against anyone, Locke declares that "the law of nature would, as all other laws concern men in this world, be in vain, if there were nobody that in the state of nature had a power to execute that law."[2] Locke's point is not the commonplace one that animals and humans had better not injure others lest they suffer retaliation; for so far there is no consideration implied of rights, the laws of nature or of men, or even punishment. It is, rather, that (a) there are rights, in the state of nature, to life, liberty, and property; that (b) these rights impose certain requirements on others to avoid invading or violating these rights, these requirements constituting the sense of the reference to the laws of nature; that (c) right holders need to be made secure in the possession and enjoyment of their rights by the right that some person or persons have to punish those who fail to meet these requirements; and that (d) given the fact that there is no central authority to impose the punishment in the state of nature, everyone has the right to punish any offender against anyone, thereby executing the law of nature. It is, then, only because there are the rights to life, liberty, and property in the state of nature that everyone has the right to punish. In the absence of these natural rights, there could be no reason for ascribing the right to punish to anyone. And so it is with other special rights such as the right established by a promise: in the absence of the rights to life, liberty, and property—this now is the reason for describing them as fundamental—there could not

2. *Second Treatise*, para. 7. Locke's view is quite different from the so-called contractarian view of John Rawls, whose view, I argue in *Rights and Persons*, is Kantian. Rawls thinks that the force of our familiar appeal to natural rights can be spelled out in terms of the claims that can be given a special weight or priority. Such claims are to be understood as those following from the principles of justice as fairness. But such principles, like Kant's fundamental principles of morality, make no reference to rights. Cf. Rawls's *A Theory of Justice* (Cambridge, Mass.: Harvard University Press, 1971), p. 505n. I discuss the parallelism between Rawls and Kant in my *Rights and Persons*, Chap. III.

be any right conferred by any promise. Locke does not make the attempt to show why this is true. But we need to remember that, like the right to punish, the rights established by a covenant made in the state of nature, as the result of which civil government is established, are not themselves natural rights. In summary, therefore, it is only because persons have certain natural rights, whether in the state of nature or in civil society, that they have any other rights.

Deficient as Mill's account of rights may be in a number of respects, including the fact that nowhere in that account do we find any distinction between natural or human rights and the variety of rights of which he does take notice, it is to his credit that, unlike Bentham, for whom there are only those rights established by statute, he does recognize the central importance of moral rights in our common conception of justice. Bentham had rejected the doctrine of natural rights to which appeal was made by the partisans of the French Revolution (an appeal clearly Lockean in origin), on the ground that it was nothing less than an invitation to anarchy, deriding it as "nonsense upon stilts."[3] But Locke's doctrine is not one of unqualified libertarianism. For if we are to describe Locke's natural rights as absolute, we must not suppose that they may be exercised arbitrarily. To say that they are absolute is simply to say that their possession is not conditional upon there being special relations or transactions between persons, as in the case of siblings or of those who obtained promises from others. It is to say, rather, that their possession depends simply and solely upon the status of persons as persons.[4] And this, clearly, is *not* to say that they may be exercised arbitrarily.

3. See his *Anarchical Fallacies.*
4. A number of passages in Locke's *Second Treatise* make it clear that on his view the fact that a right is absolute does not imply that it may be exercised arbitrarily. But he does waffle. In para. 8 he writes that although men have the power or right to punish those who invade their natural rights, this right is not an "absolute or arbitrary" right to deal with offenders "according to the passionate heats, or boundless extravagancy of [their] will." But notice that, as in our expres-

My concern, however, has not been not to defend Locke's doctrine of natural rights but to remove misconceptions about that doctrine, and thereby to prepare the way for an account of the differences between the role of rights talk in early discussions of justice and in our own. For this reason I turn now to recent talk about human rights.

In no small measure because of the misunderstanding created by Bentham's vigorous attack on the essentially Lockean doctrine of natural rights that revolutionaries in France called "the rights of man," talk about the natural rights in the philosophical literature largely faded away. Some sporadic attempts to make sense of this talk were made in the decades prior to World War II, but not until the horrors

---

sion "power or right" the function of "or" is not to present an alternative to power but to mark the sense in which this term is used, so in Locke's use of the expression "absolute or arbitrary," the words "or arbitrary" merely serve to elucidate what is meant by "absolute." It is by no means clear, however, that Locke generally thinks of "absolute" as meaning arbitrary. For even where, as in paras. 23, 171, and 172, Locke is thinking about the arbitrary powers of slave owners and depots and speaks of "absolute, arbitrary power," this expression would be oddly redundant if by "absolute" Locke meant arbitrary. And Locke is explicit in distinguishing between absolute and arbitrary when he tells us, in para. 139, that "the prince, or senate . . . can never have a power to take to themselves the whole, or any part of the subject's property, without their own consent: for this would be in effect to leave them no property at all. . . . [L]et us see, that even absolute power, where it is necessary, is not arbitrary by being absolute, but is still limited by that reason," etc. And he goes on to present the analogy between the sovereign and the military commander in the field: an army requires for its preservation "absolute obedience to the command of every superior officer"; but there are limits to the obedience owed the commander, who cannot command any soldier "to give him one penny of his money." So there are limits to the obedience a subject owes his sovereign; the latter cannot play the despot in the requirements he imposes upon his subjects. Here it is quite clear that "absolute" is used in contrast with "conditional"; the commander may withhold money from his inferiors only if they have given him specific authority—with their explicit consent—to do so; but no such consent is required for the authority of the commander in the field to order his troops to advance to their certain death. So, too, with the sovereign who cannot take the property of any of his subjects unless specific or special authority to do so has been given him.

The truth is that Locke is often careless in his use of "absolute," and this, together with Bentham's diatribe, has led many, who might have been expected to read Locke's text with care, to ascribe to Locke the silly view that there are natural rights that may be exercised as one wills, no matter what the circumstances may be.

perpetrated by the Nazis were widely publicized was there any serious and sustained effort by philosophers to take seriously some such idea as that there are indeed certain rights that human beings or persons have simply by virtue of their status as human beings or persons. It will be useful, in order to show the extent to which changes have occurred in our thinking about natural or human rights, to consider some of the items listed in the *Universal Declaration of Human Rights*, adopted in 1948 by the General Assembly of the United Nations.

The list is a curious one—a mixed bag as it were—for in addition to the Lockean rights to life, liberty, and property, a wide variety of items are said to be human rights. Here are only a few:

The right to freedom of movement and residence within the boundaries of each state.

The right to equal pay for equal work.

The right to rest and leisure, including reasonable limitations on working hours, and periodic holidays with pay.

The right to opportunity for education.

The right to adequate measures for the maintenance of health.

And so on for the thirty Articles of the document—a variety of moral desiderata are presented toward which, unfortunately, no member state, including our own, has fully bent its efforts.

Can we suppose, however, that there is a right that all of us have, one that follows from our status as human beings, to equal pay for equal work? How can a right to anything that depends for its existence upon the fact that there is some specific institution—or, for that matter, some specific arrangement of any sort in which human beings may or may not conduct themselves—be said to be a matter of *human* right, one that follows from our common status as human beings? One might as well say that there are, among other *human* rights, the right acquired by means of a promise to some help, for oneself or anyone else, as in the case of certain second-person or third-person promises.

We seem to be faced with a dilemma: either most of the so-called rights listed in the *Universal Declaration* are not human rights at all, or if they are human rights, their status as human rights depends not on our common human nature but only on the fact, perhaps, that they are particularly important, that, as John Rawls put it, they are to be given special weight.[5] If we adopt the latter alternative, the qualifying adjective "human" would appear to be misleading, and all the talk about "human rights" involves a radical change from the traditional doctrine of human or natural rights.

What does it mean to say that a human right is particularly important or that it is to be given special weight? Any right, given the appropriate circumstances, can be as important if not more so than any other competing right; and if, on the grounds of their importance, we designate rights as human rights, we had better not withhold that title from any kind of right. No right is sacrosanct. Shall we say that the right to life, because of its importance, always, even in the case of one who preys on the weak and the helpless, takes precedence over *any* other rights, even the special rights of victims, no matter what the circumstances may be? Besides, shall we say that any moral right, human or not, *must* take precedence over any other type of consideration no matter what the case may be? If we had to choose between the very survival of some Tom, Dick, and Harry and providing the help needed by some aspiring Rembrandt or Da Vinci to bring his talents to fruition, must one opt for the former? Finally, the *Universal Declaration* lists, among other rights, those peculiarly relevant to the conditions of a modern industrial society. But, given the record of the recent industrial developments that have taken place as more and

5. *A Theory of Justice*, p. 505n.

more sophisticated electronic gadgets have been devised for the efficient production of goods and services, why should we believe that a complete list of all such rights can be prepared now for all time in the future? For example, in view of the increasing use of electronic devices why not include, among other putative human rights, the right to very frequent rest periods, to changes of job routine, etc., in order to cope effectively with the increasing problem of eye fatigue induced by staring at electronic screens? Might not the air traffic controllers who were summarily dismissed by presidential fiat have complained several years ago that their human rights had been violated by the conditions of their employment? There would seem to be no end to the sorts of things that could be claimed to be human rights, if these are to be tied to the particular conditions of any given time and place, as indeed they were by the authors of the *Universal Declaration*. Yet we do think of human rights as those that depend on our common human status, a status that remains fairly constant despite the changes that have been, and even now are, taking place in our institutions, practices, and the production of goods and services.

Suppose, however, we decide to restrict our fundamental rights to those we have by virtue of our common human nature, regardless of the social conditions of any given time and place, in the way in which the supporters of the doctrine of natural rights traditionally did. Are we now to dismiss the claims made in the *Universal Declaration* as inflated rhetoric that serves only to emphasize the importance in our society of the measures we need to take in order to implement the human rights we do have? If we take this line, and restrict our fundamental human rights to life, liberty, and the pursuit of happiness, or as I have done elsewhere, to the pursuit of one's interests, then we shall have to think of education, periodic vacations with pay, etc., not as matters to which anyone has a right as a human being, but as matters that persons must have if they are to exercise and enjoy the fundamental rights they do have. It would be pointless to assert that human beings as such have the rights to life and liberty, or to the pursuit of their interests, but wholly ignore the measures that need to be taken to implement these rights, just as it would be offensive, to say the least, to concede that a person has certain rights as a human being but deny that person any opportunity to exercise them. What indeed would be the point of having any right without having any opportunity to exercise it? In particular, what would be the point of having a human right, whether it be the right to life and liberty, or even more generally to the pursuit of one's interests, without the benefits of an education, satisfactory working conditions, adequate housing, etc.? For these benefits enable one to exercise and enjoy these rights, and, in the right to pursue one's interest, to develop the interests of which one is capable and to exercise them and achieve for oneself, and for others to whom one is bound, those goods that make one's life and their's worth living? Shall we say that proper working conditions, periodic holidays with pay, etc., while not themselves matters to which persons have rights as human beings, are important only because in their absence we could not exercise and enjoy the human rights we do have?

If we took this line, we could, evidently, avoid what seems to be the exaggerated rhetoric of the *Universal Declaration*, a rhetoric that results from the conflation of two issues: the one pertaining to the human rights that persons have as the human beings they are, and the other to the specific circumstances, the settings as it were, in which these rights, which all persons have in common whoever, whenever, and wherever they may be, may be exercised and enjoyed. On this account of the matter, declarations of human rights must be made only in general terms, in terms that apply to persons whatever the special circumstances of their lives may be. In contrast, the measures necessary to implement these rights need to be specified in order to take due account of the particular, variable, and changing conditions of human life.

The issue here is analogous to the one that has arisen recently in discussions of American constitutional law. The Constitution, a written document, sets forth, and in general terms, a number of fundamental rights. The authors of this document were deliberate in doing so, leaving it to posterity to decide how these rights were to be employed. Quite recently, the attorney general of the United States questioned the ruling of the Supreme Court, in the Miranda case, that anyone accused of a crime must be informed of his or her right to remain silent. The attorney general's ground was that the framers of the Constitution had nothing of this sort in mind when they wrote that no one could be compelled to testify against oneself.

What the authors of the document had in mind may very well have been restricted to the inadmissibility of confessions obtained by threats of bodily harm or by torture; but this is not to the point. For in fact the framers of the Constitution laid down quite general guidelines, leaving it to others to decide, as new and unforeseen circumstances arose, how best to apply them. Of course the framers had nothing in mind like the use of more recently devised psychological techniques involving prolonged interrogation, suggestion, etc., commonly called "brainwashing." They had no way of foreseeing the possibility that there could be the sorts of "confessions" that were obtained by Stalin's underlings and used in the infamous public trials of the 1930s. But this does not imply that, in ruling as they did in the Miranda case— and as they should in the case of any confession obtained from those who are so terrorized while under police custody that they will agree to confess to virtually anything, or in the case of those subjected to equally effective psychological influences who confess to crimes they may or may not have committed—the justices were in effect amending the Constitution. The justices were not implying by their rulings that they could discern in the writings of this document the invisible but genuine intentions of its framers, when the latter declared that no one may be forced to testify against oneself. It was *because* of this constitutional right that the justices wisely ruled as they did in the Miranda case.[6]

And so it is in case of our natural or human rights: it is *because* of one's human rights to life and liberty, or, more generally stated, the pursuit of one's interests, that provision should be made for proper housing, working conditions, equal opportunities of education, etc. But does it follow from this that in addition to these rights there are all of the wide variety of rights listed in all of the articles of the *Universal Declaration?* That would appear to necessitate rewriting our fundamental moral constitution whenever important changes in our institutions and practices occur that require us to include new fundamental rights.

Persuasive as these considerations may be, I am not convinced, as I was in the past, that paying proper attention, in the changing social conditions of our lives, to such matters as adequate working conditions, periodic holidays with pay, etc., which are tied to special circumstances, is merely a matter of what ought to be done rather than a matter of human right—of implementing rather than expanding the list of our human rights. Consider the legal analogy. We do in fact say of the person in police custody, who is suspected of having committed a criminal act, that he has a constitutional right to remain silent, even though the Constitution says nothing about such a right. And much has been said

6. The view set forth here is now familiar enough. Ronald Dworkin, in *Taking Rights Seriously* (Cambridge, Mass.: Harvard University Press, 1977), Chap. V, provides an admirably detailed argument in support of it during the course of his critical examination of "strict constructionism." He describes the statements of fundamental rights in the Constitution as vague; I prefer to use the word "general," my thoughts being that what the framers of that document deliberately and wisely did was to leave unstated the *specific* circumstances to which the general statement was to be applied by those who would follow them.

in recent years about the violation of human rights in the Soviet Union and in South Africa when these governments deny persons the right to emigrate, move freely within their boundaries, or reside wherever they choose to do so—the sorts of things the *Universal Declaration* declares to be matters of human right. For to deny persons these sorts of things is to deny them, as residents of these states, the right they have to pursue their interests and to liberty, rights that strike us as being part of our fundamental moral constitution.

Let it be, therefore, that the right to proper working conditions is conceptually linked to the notion of labor as a commodity to be exchanged for the money or the goods necessary for survival—matters that are tied to the special circumstances of given times and places. It does not follow that proper working conditions are merely matters that ought to be provided those persons in the relevant and special circumstances and are not, therefore, matters to which these persons have a right as human beings. For if I have, as a fundamental right, the right to pursue interests of which I am capable, and thereby to achieve for myself or for others the goods these define, then, given that the goods and services needed for the exercise of this right are normally available in the special conditions of social existence of a given time and place, I have a right to those goods and services. And if I am denied those needed goods and services, I am denied the right that I have as a human being.[7] Given, then, social circumstances like the existence of factories for the production of goods, if I have a right to things appropriate to my particular status as a worker in a factory, I have a

---

7. What shall we say about circumstances in which the things needed for the exercise of one's right are much too scarce to go around, as in the case of an imaginary but quite possible nuclear fall and subsequent nuclear winter? Do persons cease to have rights in such conditions of extreme scarcity? How much point is there in using the complex language of moral rights in circumstances in which any exercise of moral rights is precluded? Indeed, what is meant by the "normal" availability of the relevant goods and services needed for the exercise of these rights? To explore these matters to any satisfactory extent would carry us beyond the limits of this essay.

right to those conditions of employment that make it possible for me to pursue the interests that factory workers, no less than others, can be presumed to have. And if I am being raised in an industrial society, then I do have a right to equal access to an education consonant with my abilities so that I can develop the interests I am capable of acquiring and live a life worth living.

There is, therefore, no objection to labeling many of the different sorts of things listed in the *Universal Declaration* as human rights, in addition to such *fundamental* rights as the rights to life and liberty. It is only because the list of human rights in that document is a mixed bag, suggesting that all the rights listed are, so to speak, on the same level, that it is open to objection. For the mistake made by the authors of the document is not that rights are conflated with the moral requirements for their exercise and enjoyment in the appropriate circumstances of human life. It is rather that the rights that are common to all persons because they are based upon a common human nature are conflated with the rights that human beings have in the special circumstances of the institutions and practices of a given time and place. The latter rights are derivative; they derive from the fundamental rights that are common to human beings, whenever and wherever they may be. But they are human rights even though they are not on a par with our fundamental human rights since, unlike the latter, they change with the changing circumstances of our social institutions and practices.

6. Animal Rights?

I

In these days, in which much has been written and said by nonphilosophers and philosophers in support of the thesis that animals have moral rights, our talk about human rights may well elicit the charge of speciesism. The charge is made with some heat by pro-animal activist, some of whom, ironically enough, have not hesitated on occasion to resort to measures that violate the legal and moral rights of human beings, just as pro-life activists, on occasion, have engaged in programs of action that threaten the lives of human beings. Is there any reason to believe that animals too have moral rights?

The question may appear to be only peripheral to the issue I have raised about the changes that have occurred in the thinking about rights, ever since the first explicit mention of them was made some centuries ago; but it does have a bearing upon the conceptual features that apply quite unproblematically at least to most human beings.

We have come a long way from the days when Cartesians could maintain in all seriousness, on the alleged ground that animals are devoid of souls, that they are wonderfully contrived machines without any of the sensitivities and sensibilities of human beings. Young animals, no less than young humans, kick up their heels in a display of animal spirits. Animals, too, taste, feel, hear, smell, and see. They suffer as humans do when starved or abused; they are frightened, even terrorized, when aware of an immediate danger to their lives. And, like humans, they have moments of enjoyment in their lives, satisfactions and pleasant experiences. Some have argued on this account that animals, like humans, have rights.

There can be no doubt that, as Hume put it, "we are bound, by the laws of humanity, to give [animals] gentle usage,"[1] or, as we would say, that we ought to treat animals humanely; but this is a far cry from ascribing moral rights to them. Some have declared that we do have duties to animals, but denied that they have moral rights,[2] the thought being that our "duties"—those described traditionally as "duties of imperfect obligation"—include, among other things, the protection and the help we ought to give sentient creatures. We ought to be humane in our treatment of animals, to be kind to them, not merely because it may help us acquire and reinforce those traits that serve us well in our moral dealings with other human beings but, first, because these traits, whether we display them in our treatment of human beings or of animals, are virtues and as such are desirable, and, second, because we ought to relieve sentient creatures, humans and animals, from distress as much as we can. Does *this* imply that animals have moral rights?

We abhor the wanton destruction of animals in the wild, those of us at any rate who find the "sport" of hunting offensive. George V is said to have achieved a record by slaughtering over two thousand birds on one of his shooting forays, but the record is also one of incredible insensitivity to the havoc he created. Does this imply that he violated the right to life of the birds he killed? Some may be inclined to think so. After all, they tell us, birds, like humans, have a right to live out their lives, to forage for food, mate, and raise their young. To what extent, if at all, is the natural

1. *An Enquiry Concerning the Principles of Morals*, Sec. III.
2. See H. J. McClosky, "Moral Rights and Animals," *Inquiry* (1979): 23–54.

condition of animal life anything like the statue of nature in which, as Locke maintained, there are moral rights—not only natural rights but those other rights that exist even in that natural condition? And here we must consider not only birds but any of the animals who are in any way sentient creatures capable of feeling pleasure or pain. To this end, we need to be reminded of some of the salient features of moral rights, features that have been brought to light during the course of our discussions of the views of Locke, Mill, and the authors of the recent *Universal Declaration of Human Rights*.

As we have seen, Locke's natural rights are fundamental rights, in the absence of which there could be no other rights, not even those others existing in the state of nature. For why punish anyone who violates one's natural rights unless the punishment serves to make us secure in the enjoyment of our natural rights, and why make and accept promises unless this promotes the enjoyment or exercise of the natural rights of those party to the transaction? But unlike natural rights, which cannot be waived, relinquished, or forfeited—for they are inseparable from one's condition as human beings—other rights, whether in the state of nature or in civil society, may be asserted, waived, relinquished, or forfeited. And one who offends another by violating the latter's rights may and should be forgiven, provided that the offender make restitutions, if possible, and indicates feelings of remorse, thereby purging himself of guilt. In this way the moral barriers between offender and offended are erased as they prepare to resume with confidence and trust their normal moral relations.

All of this implies incomparably more than the capacity to feel pain; it implies that pains can be the pangs of remorse felt by one who has committed an offense against another. It implies incomparably more than the fact that persons are capable of pleasures; it implies that pleasures can be occasioned by the moral conduct of those who meet their obli-

gations to them. What is involved is their capacity to have
feelings not merely of rage or anger but also of guilt and of
gratitude toward someone who forgives one for a moral trespass. In all of this there is a great deal more than the per-
ception of the source of the one's sufferings and the retaliation it provokes, or the source of one's pleasures and
comforts provided by someone else, because of which one
displays something resembling gratitude, as in the case of
dogs who lick the hands of those who comfort and feed
them. For there is also the recognition by the individuals
concerned of their status as members of a moral community
with a shared understanding of the sorts of reasons that
impel them (a) to waive their rights or to refuse, because of
their special circumstances, to meet their obligations; (b) to
relinquish them on occasion when they are morally required
to do so; and (c) to make amends, in ways that accord with
their understanding of what they are able to do, and to offer
explanations and excuses that manifest their sensitivity to
the needs, interests, sensibilities, and temperaments of those
against whom they have trespassed. Further, members of the
moral community are (d) capable of a whole range of mental
acts in which moral agents engage during their normal activities, when they are mindful of the moral relations in
which they stand up one another—they expect, hope for,
and repose confidence in the future behavior of others when
mutual understandings are created, tacitly or expressly as
the case maybe—and (e) care about others, not merely those
who are close to one but also those outside one's immediate
circle—for how else would it be possible for persons to conduct themselves in the varying ways we have described? And
this list is by no means complete, for we could mention still
other features involved in the possession and recognition of
rights and obligations.

Can this complex and variegated conceptual structure be
extracted from the idea of a pleasure or pain that can be
ascribed to living creatures ranging from human beings

down to the bluebottle fly feeding on a piece of rotting flesh or a worm burrowing its way through the soil? For flies and worms exhibit their characteristic forms of pain behavior; and presumably even they enjoy the material upon which they feed. It matters not whether the attempt to ground rights on the fact that sentient beings are capable of pleasure and pain takes the Millian form or one that simply reduces the claim that A has a right to x to the statement that providing x to A is pleasant, withholding it is painful. In either case far, far more is required in order to ascribe rights to sentient beings.

Nor will the alleged intrinsic value of the lives of sentient beings, and the inference made to the claim that we are to respect such beings, suffice as a satisfactory account of the matter. For this view, like Kant's view that rational nature is an end in itself—a consideration that some philosophers have supposed to be an adequate ground for the ascription of rights to human beings—is intelligible not for what is alleged to be its positive content but for the sorts of things it proscribes. Presumably we are not to inflict pain and suffering upon any sentient creature, for example, to pull the wings off flies in order to observe the 'curious' way in which they thrash about. And in the case of Kant's account of morality, the respect that we ought to pay any person is the respect we are to pay any rational being, a respect that proscribes the immorality involved in acting unlawfully, in a way that consists, Kant tells us, in acting on maxims we are not prepared to make universal laws for all rational beings. Why not? Because, he tells us, rational nature exists as an end in itself or has an intrinsic value. But whatever does this mean? Here we are told not what this value consists in but in what this value rules out, among other things the treatment of persons as if they were things with their prices, to be used, replaced by their equivalents, or discarded when they no longer serve our purposes.

The obscurity is compounded by Kant's declaration that

the different forms of the principle of the categorical imperative are equivalent, in consequence of which it would appear that acting on a maxim one is not prepared to universalize is demeaning oneself by not acting as a rational being, a being that has intrinsic value, but as a being subject to the idiosyncratic force of inclination. However, if treating anyone else as a being with intrinsic value is to be *equivalent* to being disposed to act on maxims that apply equally to oneself and everyone else, it is difficult to understand what is meant by the claim that anyone, including oneself, has intrinsic value, other than this, that everyone ought to be treated equally, that everyone counts morally.

But this demand for equality or fairness is not the demand that rights ought to be respected. And nowhere in his account of the three forms of the principle of the categorical imperative or in the proof or "deduction" he gives us does Kant make any reference to rights, and wisely so. Indeed, the current widespread idea that Kant thought he was expounding, in his account of the treatment one ought to give either oneself or anyone else, anything that has to do with rights, is only evidence of the fashionable tendency to engage in morally inflated rhetoric by supposing that there is a right whenever there is an ought—by supposing, to consider an extreme example, that since one ought to protect the environment, the latter, along with human and other animals, has its rights.

But the fact that one ought to give persons equal treatment does not entail that they have a *right* to such treatment. If, gratuitously, I distribute candies to a group of youngsters with whom I am not acquainted, it would be manifestly unfair if, capriciously, I gave some of them more than I gave others, and thereby failed to give the rest of them anything at all. But there is no moral right involved here, however much those I neglect may have had, as we commonly put it, a right to expect, as I was doling out the candies, that they too would receive their fair or equal share; for none of them had any right to any of the candies.

Let us return now to the claim that any sentient creature, great or small, human or nonhuman, has an intrinsic value, that because of this we ought to respect it, and that therefore any sentient being possesses rights—minimally, the right to life itself. What indeed can be meant by the "intrinsic value" of any animal? Is this something that it has all by itself, no matter what else may be the case, even if, as G. E. Moore once thought, it were to exist in total isolation? Is this intrinsic value something that can be understood only by being apprehended by the mind's eye, in some flesh of intuition? If not, some explanation is surely needed.

Furthermore, what is meant by the "respect" we ought to pay any living creature—the bluebottle fly, earthworm, pheasant, dolphin, ape, or human being—is by no means clear. We understand well enough what is meant by saying that we ought to respect John's rights even when John is a scoundrel, a person for whom, as we commonly say, we *have* no respect. That at least can be spelled out in terms of, among other things, the role rights do or should play in our moral dealings even with a person we do not respect at all. But the respect that is said to be due *any* living creature is something else again. Is it that one ought to deal fairly with any animal just as one ought to deal fairly with human beings—treating animals on terms of equality with human beings? One ought not to treat animals as if they were insensitive to pain and suffering, but this is not to say that we ought to deal with them on terms of equality with human beings. Still less is it to say that we ought to treat them as moral agents, with a respect for their moral rights. If we are to find good reasons for ascribing rights to animals, we had better look elsewhere.

I shall not review here a variety of other considerations—such as the fact that animals have needs, desires, or interests—that have been adduced as grounds for the ascription of rights. Nor need I comment specifically on recent proposals to include trees, streams, and the other items in the total environment of human and animal life as bearers of moral rights. All such attempts must fail unless the notion of a moral right is so weakened that saying, for example, that trees have moral rights is only a confused and confusing way of saying that we ought to provide proper conditions for their growth and survival. But so to weaken or dilute the import or the ascription of moral rights would be not only to ignore the distinctive features of such rights; it would also reduce the question whether the ancients thought that trees had moral rights—surely a bizarre question—to the eminently sensible question whether they thought that trees ought to be preserved and, where possible, given adequate conditions for their nurture.

It would be futile to attempt to support the view that animals, plants, etc., have moral rights on the ground that we, individually or collectively, have no right to harm or damage them; for it simply does not follow from the fact that we have no right to do these things to the entities in question that they have rights against us. We have no right to do any number of different things where no question of rights is at issue, where the only consideration is that the act in question fails to meet a so-called duty of imperfect obligation, such as the requirement that we be kind to others, and polite and generous in our dealings with them. There are all sorts of reasons for doing things that involve no consideration of rights. We ought to protect the environment, cleanse the air and our oceans, lakes, and streams, protect our forests and wilderness areas, etc., for aesthetic, economic, and recreational reasons, concern for future generations, etc., without appealing to rights of animals, plants, and inanimate entities. We should put a stop to cruelty to animals because it *is* cruel, relieve their suffering because they *are* suffering, feed the starving elk in winter because they are unable to forage for food, and so on. One need not be an animal rights advocate in order to support one's local Humane Society. And there are choices, sometimes hard ones, that need to be made. Are we to refrain from the use of animals for medical research if this is the only way we can advance medical science? And if we turn vegetarian in order to avoid trespassing on the 'sacred' rights of animals, we should recognize that the cost of bringing virgin lands into cultivation and protecting crops raised for our consumption is a heavy one for animals; the animals who nibble away at the crops, and the insects that prey on the fruit of the soil, are fair game to the farmer.

II

Why then have philosophers and nonphilosophers, too, claimed, not without passion, that animals have their rights, that even inanimate objects have their moral rights? There are, I believe, two main reasons; and here, of course, I ignore religious doctrines.

First, there are the heavy overtones of rights talk, in comparison with which the talk about what ought to be done might seem to be relatively pallid. Saying that animals have a right to the care we can give them seems to be more effective in summoning our efforts on their behalf than saying that we ought to care for them.

Second, and much more interesting, there has been a growing recognition in recent years that some important traits formerly thought to be exclusively human are also displayed by certain animals. Research by animal psychologists has shown that some animals seem to use tools and language, and display intelligence in hitherto unexpected, albeit limited, ways. One consequence of this fact, it should be noted in passing, is that those who have attempted, erroneously in my opinion, to find a basis for moral rights in our common rationality are hard put not only to find room for the rights of human beings of subnormal intelligence but also to offer good reason for denying them to the great apes, chimpanzees, whales and, among others, porpoises.[3] We have learned, too, in recent days that animals like the great apes and the huge whales are not the fearsome and intractable beasts of popular legend but creatures who care for each other in their own social groups. We have also learned that, given gentle and encouraging treatment by sensitive human beings, they can respond with curiosity, playfulness, and even affection. In addition to this new scientific knowledge there is the old and familiar story about man's best friend, and other pets as well. They can be affectionate, caring, protective of the homes in which they live and of their occupants, grief-stricken at the loss of their masters, dignified and confident members of the household, sensitive to the demands of their masters—in short, individuals with their distinctive personalities, who have a place in the family households. These are the substantive considerations that have led some to ascribe moral rights to at least some members of the nonhuman animal kingdom.

But there are certain concerns we have about animals, other than that concern we have to relieve them of their suffering, which are quite different from anything involved in our family pets; and I shall discuss some of these before returning to a consideration of the argument for ascribing rights to our pets. Consider, to begin with, the incident that occurred not long ago in which the permission to construct a dam in the southwestern part of the United States was denied on the ground that it was far more important to preserve a rare species of fish inhabiting the few remaining pools in the riverbed than to increase the water supply for human inhabitants in the surrounding arid area. Some may have thought that the decision was based on the recognition

3. For a radical departure from popular views, past ones at least, concerning the 'human' characteristics of many animals, the reader should consult Mary Midgley's *Beast and Man* (Ithaca, N.Y.: Cornell University Press, 1978).

by the authorities of the right to life of the fish, but such an inference would have been mistaken. What the authorities were concerned about was the preservation of the *species*, not the lives of a few individual fish. For had there been many other members of that particular species, not only in that particular area but elsewhere in and outside the country, there would have been no compunction on the part of the authorities in allowing human beings to kill the few fish in the pools of that particular riverbed. It was, presumably, with a view to the preservation of that particular species, out of concern to prevent any damage to one important facet of the economy of nature, that permission for the construction of the dam was denied.

And when statutes were established not long ago imposing what might appear to be unusually heavy fines for the killing of condors in California, the fines were imposed not for killing any specific member of the species but for acting in a way that was likely to lead to the extinction of the species. The right to life is a right that an individual animal, human or nonhuman, has; but in the present instance the killing of a particular animal is of concern to us because it is a threat to the species as a whole. And the threat to the species is what concerns us precisely because of our interest in seeing to it that the result of an evolutionary development that plays an important role in the economy of nature is preserved, even at the cost of short-term benefits to be gained by the killing of a few animals.

Consider next the case of the flip remark of a former governor of California, now president of the United States, who brushed aside the efforts of environmentalists to preserve the state's redwood forests in the face of the persistent attempts of the lumber industry to gain access to them, declaring "When you've seen one tree, you've seen them all." This, among other things, is to ignore the vast difference between the awesome and inspiring view of redwood trees

towering above one in the stillness of a forest and the lum-
berman's myopic vision of the trees as so much lumber to
be produced and sold at a profit. The flip remark was symptomatic of nothing less than a callousness that prevented the
then-governor from seeing a redwood forest as anything
other than "a lot of trees" about which too much of a fuss
was being made by what he no doubt thought was a bizarre
group of strident "activists." We have no need to appeal to
the moral rights of trees in order to argue for the preservation of forests, and we have no need to appeal to the
moral rights of the fish in order to argue that we should
preserve the species. Not only is there no need, it is at the
very least questionable that this borrowing of rights talk
from the area of human interaction in which it does have
its place to the case of the small fish in a pool or the case
of the trees is intellectually responsible.

There are other cases to be considered. Some elderly and
lonely people have goldfish, canaries, cats, and dogs as pets,
and lavish their affection upon them and enjoy their companionship. What a pity it is when the pets die! But they
are replaceable. And there is none of the grief felt when a
member of the family dies. Another case: When I approach
the koi in my garden pool, they observe me and move rap-
idly to the end of the pool where they are accustomed to
receive their food. I know only too well that they come to
me not out of affection or friendship but because they are
hungry. They are, in fact, quite stupid; but I keep them and
care for them because they are decorative.

A much more interesting case is that of the stag I see in
the wild, a magnificent animal, proud and defiant as he
herds his females. I do respect him, not as a moral agent
with whom I can conduct my affairs, supporting his agency
as he would mine, nor as one to whose interests I must give
due consideration out of any sense of fairness, but because
he is a magnificent member of the animal kingdom—strong,
virile, commanding, caring toward and protective of his

harem. He is a noble beast that must be seen to be appreciated, not as so much meat to be hung in one's locker or stored in a freezer but as the truly remarkable product of evolutionary development that he is. Some who are particularly struck by these qualities of the animal understandably are moved to employ rhetoric that emphasizes the respects in which he is similar to us. Biologically, he does have much in common with us. We are his kith if not his kin. He is a fellow passenger on Spaceship Earth. And so on with other locutions that focus upon features we share with him—but that all too frequently ignore the respects in which we are importantly different from him and other members of his species. For however much we have in common with this creature, appreciate and admire him, we do differ from him in ways that are, morally speaking, of great importance and that preclude the ascription of rights that as I shall argue below, might well be ascribed to a few special cases of animals.

Nevertheless, some will insist that animals like our magnificent stag, along with the laboratory rat employed in experiments, can be said to have rights. For they can and do suffer, and they do have interests, some if not many of which they have in common with human beings. Why not say, on this ground alone, that they do have rights, albeit in a different sense of the term, one that is far more dilute than the familiar sense in which we have employed the term?

There are, it seems to me, two very good reasons for not doing this. First, it is quite unnecessary to do so, for there are substantial considerations, quite independent of rights, that can be invoked against cruelty to animals, the willful slaughter of animals in the wild, and the barbarous practices of the hunt, and extinction of species, as well as the pollution of the environment and the depletion of our forests. Second, this new way with the word "rights," designed as it is to borrow the heavy overtones of rights talk, can be, and indeed has proved to be, mischievous. For words, despite Humpty Dumpty's principle that we are master over them and not the other way round, have a way of mastering us because of our habituation to their familiar usages. The use of talk about rights in order to provide rhetorical emphasis to the importance of the considerations I have mentioned, which in themselves provide sufficient grounds for denouncing certain treatments of animals, is likely to lead us on to the supposition that animal rights, so-called, are like human rights. Some indeed have actually supposed that these offenses against animals are on a par with the offenses against human beings if the latter were, for example, to be kept locked up in cages and exhibited in a zoo or subjected against their will to painful treatment in laboratory experiments. There are good and sufficient reasons of the sort I have reviewed to deter us from offensive conduct toward animals, without our resorting to talk about rights, which often opens the way to confusion and even fanaticism.[4]

But it should be remarked, parenthetically, that the ascription of moral rights, in the sense with which I have been concerned, to very special cases of, say, the canine member of the family and perhaps some few members of the animal kingdom, such as the whale and the porpoise, is far removed from any argument or plea for vegetarianism to which, as I mentioned earlier, a general ascription of rights to animals can lead. For even granted that the animals mentioned have moral rights, this does not establish that all animals do. And even if we grant that all animals have rights, it does not follow that one must abstain from using animals as food. For rights, even our fundamental rights, as Locke saw long ago, are not absolute in that absurd sense of the term in which they may never be overridden no matter what the circumstances are. We might well have to choose between

4. The preceding four paragraphs were prompted by a question raised by Allen Buchanan in comments about my discussion of the ascription of rights to special cases of animals in that familiar sense of the word "right" with which I have been concerned in this essay.

the rights of humans and those of animals; indeed, as I observed earlier, the efficient use of agricultural land raises havoc with living creatures who prey upon crops. And if the world population continues to grow at an every-increasing rate, we may well have to choose between using living creatures as a source of food and starving to death.

Let us now return to the special cases of pets, among certain other animals, and ask whether their special features establish that they have moral rights. To begin with, we should be careful not to misread their behavior. For instance, when a dog has soiled the carpet and moves stealthily away with its tail between its legs, we might well be in error in supposing that this is not fear of being discovered and spanked but the recognition of its guilt in breaching a mutual understanding established between itself and its master. And we should be careful not to misread its anger, when someone prevents it from eating its meal, as the moral indignation of a being whose rights to its food have been violated. But there are dogs that behave in ways that incline us to say that they are members of the family, that they and their masters have mutual expectations about the ways in which the dogs may behave, mutual expectations of the sort that are very much like those involved in tacit promises. Such dogs seem to have their own individual personalities, and they seem to be able to discriminate between the personalities of the human beings in the family. The dog may exhibit the behavior of puzzlement when a human member of the family deprives it of what it has good reason to expect, and it may seem to demand its rights when there is no food in its dish. We are inclined to say in these cases that behavior appropriate to one who has rights is as evident as the pain behavior of a fly that twists to and fro when injured. To be sure, a dog cannot declare that it waives its rights or that it relinquishes them. But just as we may be inclined to say that it demands its right to food when it clamors for it, so we may say that it seems to waive it when it submits to the deprivation. There is much more than this in the lives of human beings who are sensible of one other's rights and obligations: they understand full well how to behave in ways that are appropriate to the moral relations in which they stand each other; they feel the variety of moral emotions that are appropriate when rights are breached and obligations are neglected; they recognize that they must make amends and offer explanations for their moral failures; and so on (here we need to be reminded of the complex conceptual structure sketched earlier). Nevertheless, the concept of a right and its correlative obligation may have at least as much of a foothold in the case of a pet dog as the concept of pain in the behavior of an injured fly.

It must be remembered that because of its normative status the complex conceptual structure of rights can be delineated only by examining what is involved in those cases in which human beings, with the requisite understanding and sensitivity, generally meet the normative requirements imposed upon them by rights—their own and those of others—or make amends, offer explanations, and so on, which are called for when they fall short of these requirements. It is by reference to the many varied cases of these sorts that we learn to understand what it is to have a moral right. But there are many human beings who in one or more respects fail to meet these requirements: the mentally handicapped, the boorish and the callous, those suffering to a greater or lesser extent from arrested or deviant moral development, the self-centered and the immoral who are all too ready to breach what they themselves recognize to be the rights of others. However, there are considerations other than moral rights that require us to act toward such people in ways that are appropriate to human beings.

Similarly, there are limits in the case of animals; for we should not ascribe moral rights to earthworms even though there are considerations other than the possession of rights that call for us to conduct ourselves toward them in ways appropriate to their behavior. But at the other end of the spectrum of cases we do find animals who seem to have some of the features of moral agents, limited as those may be, and to whom we are inclined to ascribe moral rights of one sort or another. And in recent days we have come to understand that it is possible to develop a rapprochement with some undomesticated members of the animal kingdom and deal with them in ways, limited as these may be, that resemble those in which rights and obligations are involved.[5]

There are undoubtedly borderline cases to which the concept of a moral right has only the most problematic application, as when there seems to be something that suggests a mutual understanding established between man and beast to live and let live, but which really amounts only to indifference or lack of fear. And some animal life does appear to have social features; but how much of this is instinctively determined in ways that do not involve the exercise of any intelligence, and how much involves something like the mutual understandings that operate where there are moral rights, it would be difficult to determine. But in the case of canine "members of the family" there does appear to be some warrant for our ascribing rights to animals, conceptually truncated as these may be.

Does this mean that we can speak in such cases of degrees of rights, that some animals at least have a lesser degree of a given right than most human beings? We can and do say that some human beings—the members of one's family— enjoy more rights than the stranger without kith or kin; but this is no reason for saying that whatever right someone does in fact have is more or less of that particular right.

5. Tongue in cheek or not, but with his characteristic denigration of democracy, in which "liberty is the noblest possession," Plato writes that "the very animals catch the infection of anarchy" in a democracy (*Republic* 562). Even Plato seems to regard it as at least intelligible to speak of the characteristic behavior of an animal infected with the spirit of anarchy, the idea that anyone *may* act as he or she pleases, an idea to be distinguished, surely, from that of a being acting on the impulse of the moment.

Neither do we, nor should we, think that whatever particular right someone has, a morally good man has it to a
greater degree than one of lesser merit. And to say that a
member of a family has a certain right against others in the
family to a greater degree than does a "member of the family" who is a pet dog, in the sense that the former right is
to be given greater weight than the latter in determining
what should be done on any given occasion, is to conflate
the role of the right in justifying conduct with its status as
a right. Certainly it will not do to think of a right as having
more or less of an existence as its degree diminishes, fading
away finally to nothingness. Having a right is not a matter
of degree in the way in which having hair on one's scalp is
a matter of degree, ranging from a full head of hair to perfect baldness; for there is no such thing as a unit feature in
the case of a right as there is in the case of hair—a single
follicle of hair—so that the more units a given right has the
greater the degree of the right.

Do we think that any given feature of a right is essential,
so that, lacking that feature, something could not be spoken
of as right? One has a right when there has been an understanding, expressed or implied, as in the case of an explicit or tacit promise; but must there be such an understanding in every case? Consider the infant who does have
a right to food, clothing, and shelter but has none of the
sorts of expectations or the understandings of an older child.
Again, should we always think that in according someone
his or her right by keeping a promise, that we are serving
the latter's interest and contributing to some specific course
of action to which the promised act (or abstention) is essential? Surely not; we may have been merely testing that
person's probity. For there are promises and promises, and
the rights and rights to which they give rise. We would not
regard the promise I insist on making to someone, who tells
me that he or she has no interest in the matter, a paradigm
case of a promise, and so too with the right that it creates.

Should one say in this case that the right is less of a right than it is in the usual case in which what is promised is a matter of importance to the promisor? Suppose, however, that I make a promise to someone who initially has no interest in my keeping it but who, as things turn out unexpectedly, realizes the importance of my keeping the promise; would the promise not have a solid right in the matter?

Again, suppose I make a promise—of the normal sort in which the person to whom I make it has an interest—but the person to whom I make it thinks that a promise is a promise, to be kept no matter what the circumstances may be: is the right of the promisee less of a right than the right of one who has achieved moral maturity and who does recognize that circumstances might well justify waiving or relinquishing it? For whether or not human beings do recognize this feature of rights, in principle they are capable of doing so. But that level of comprehension may never be realized by animals, not even the higher primates and our family pets. We do develop mutual understandings and expectations with them, but they incline us to say that they have a level of comprehension that exists in intelligent but very morally insensitive human beings, beings who seem to have no sense of the fact that rights are not like bank notes payable simply on demand. But even in the case of human beings we find more or less of the understanding of the complexity of the features in terms of which our concept of a right is to be elucidated; yet we do not say on that account that the right a human being has is a matter of degree. And we do not say about mentally retarded humans, who are incapable of grasping the full complexity of our concept of a right, that they have rights to a lesser degree than those who are morally more sophisticated.

There is one further point that must be made in this connection. Philosophers sometimes employ what may be dubbed "the slippery slope argument" in denying, for example, that infants have moral rights. What is to stop us, they ask, from claiming that fetuses, even newly fertilized ova, have moral rights? It is not possible here to examine the complicated tangle of questions relating to abortion. Neither is it possible here to discuss the question whether newly born infants have moral rights, a question to which an affirmative answer for a variety of different reasons has been given.[6]

Instead, I shall concern myself with the question whether or not we are sliding down the slope—toward who knows what—once we concede not only that the morally mature and sensitive but also, and in varying degrees, that the growing but not yet matured young person has moral rights. The answer, surely, to the question whether there is anything to stop our slide into allegedly patent absurdity, is our good common sense in the matter. And if, in reply, it is asked where and how we can draw the line between beings—human or animal—who have moral rights and those who do not, once more the response is that it is only good sense in the matter that tells us that no such line need or can be drawn. So it is with animal rights. The demand that we must be able to give a flat-out "Yes" or "No" answer to the question whether any creature, human or animal, has moral rights, must be rejected. What is important is not that such an answer be given in every case, but how it is that we are to deal with animals or human beings in ways that are appropriate to their particular condition, whatever it may happen to be.

6. Some have asserted that because infants are potential adult human beings of some requisite degree of moral maturity, they have moral rights. But this alleged ground only establishes that potentially they have moral rights. Others contend that they have the right to an open future and, therefore, the right to whatever is required for their development into adult human beings who, unproblematically, do have moral rights. In my *Rights and Persons* I take a different approach. I argue that infants are human beings in their infancy and that as human beings in their infancy they have a right to life, the point being that the moral status of the infant is no more to be tied to its particular condition during the human being's infancy than the moral status of one who is asleep or unconscious is to be tied to its condition at the time it is asleep or unconscious.

Wise parents know well enough that they must "grow up," so to speak, with their children, altering their expectations of, demands on, and attitudes and conduct toward their children as the latter slowly grow to moral, social, and intellectual maturity, in ways that are not only appropriate to their particular condition at the time but also likely to elicit their best efforts to take further steps toward maturity. In the case of animals what is important is not that we draw a line between those animals that do and those that do not have rights but how we are to deal with the many sorts of cases that are more and more problematic as we see less and less of the characteristic forms of rights behavior[7] in animals with which we are familiar. And, with all due caution, especially in the case of creatures in the wild, we should not only adjust our attitudes and responses to their particular condition but, in some cases, be prepared for the possibility that we have underestimated their own ability to respond to us in ways that resemble those of creatures that do engage in rights behavior. As in the case of the child whom we deal with in ways appropriate to someone somewhat older, in order to encourage it to live up to a level of maturity it has not yet achieved, so in the case of some animals, with all due caution and regard for their native endowments, we ought to deal with them in ways most likely to elicit from

---

7. I use this technical term to refer to those characteristic forms of behavior that serve as grounds for the ascription of rights to animals. We distinguish, for example, between the disobedient pet that is fearful of its master's disfavor or punishment and the pet that seems to recognize that it is guilty of a transgression and solicits its master's forgiveness. And we recognize, too, the humanlike behavior of the family pet in defending members of the household when they are under attack or in danger of losing their lives through fire, drowning, etc. Here it is not always the behavior viewed in isolation that warrants the ascription of rights but the background information we have about the dog's association with other members of the family. For a dog's movements away from the mess it has made on the carpet, with its tail between its legs, and the supplicative behavior of the dog do not always count in favor of attributing to it a sense of guilt and a desire to be forgiven. More information is needed about the way the dog has been involved in the life of the family, including the ways in which it has been dealt with when it has misbehaved, before it may be determined that in the present instance there is rights behavior.

them behavior resembling not that of intractable beasts but that of creatures to whom we are indeed inclined to ascribe rights. For in these sorts of cases we should desire to permit them to enjoy certain goods like food, shelter, and the particular forms of their social animal existence, not out of kindness or a sense of kinship, or from an interest in conserving the contribution that animals make to nature but from a sense of the rights they have. What is essential if we are to be reasonable in our views about animals rights is more information about the lives of animals, especially those higher forms of animals—who all too frequently we have supposed to be devoid of any of the sensibilities of human beings and who understandably respond in kind to the atrocious treatment we have given them in the past—lest our preconceptions about them blind us to the capacities they have to engage in better forms of conduct.[8]

8. Mention should be made of the change that has occurred in our treatment of whales. Along the coastal waters of California, where they are no longer treated as fodder for floating food factories, they respond in kind to the friendly curiosity of whale watchers who go out from shore to observe them during their migrations. They show none of the legendary ferocity of the monsters of the deep.

7. Analysis or Change?

In chapter 1, the response to the question whether the Greeks had any conception of moral rights was hedged with a number of cautions. It was argued that the fact that they had no equivalent for the term we use to designate the moral property of agents as distinct from the moral quality of actions should not be considered a decisive reason for asserting that they had no such notion at all. But, we argued, neither should it be dismissed as an irrelevant accident of linguistic fact; for the use of a new word often serves at least to bring together a number of ideas in ways that serve some particular interest. It was noted, in connection with the first mention of rights during the late medieval period, that the change in vocabulary occurred along with a new and developing sense of the importance of the freedom of the individual, however bound up this may have been with notions of natural law, and however right holders were limited to a relatively few privileged members of society: first, the members of a restive nobility, and later, the members of an emerging middle class. In the course of our discussion of the views of Locke and Mill (which deserve the extended discussion given them, not only because of their intrinsic interest but also because of prevalent obscurities and misconceptions about them) further conceptual features involved in the talk about rights emerged. The discussion turned next to the current and now popular talk about human rights, in order to focus attention upon recent developments in the role of rights in moral affairs. Finally, an attempt was made,

during the course of a discussion of animal rights, to show
that some of the conceptual features of rights, which apply
unproblematically to human beings to whom we do ascribe
rights, may in special cases apply to animals. As with human
beings, we find with animals a spectrum of cases ranging
from special instances in which the talk about rights makes
sense to borderline cases and finally to those very many cases
in which any notion of a moral right has no purchase at all.

During the course of this extended discussion, care was
taken to avoid the use of locutions like "the concept of a
right," which suggest or imply that somehow we have ar-
rived at some objective truth about the analysis of a concept,
that somehow progress has been made in avoiding the errors
of the past attempts to provide such an analysis. The concept
of a right, whether it be that of the recipient of a promise
or that of human beings as such, as we have come to think
of it during the course of the preceding discussion, may be
better than that advanced by previous thinkers. But are we
to think that "better" has any reference to the kind of objective reality and standard of the sort Plato, for example,
thought he had achieved, when in the *Republic*, after an
extended discussion of the topic, he declared that he has
discovered "the true nature of justice"? Our issue is not
whether Plato's doctrine of Forms is correct but rather
whether, as Plato did in his discussion of justice in the individual and the state, we are to think that because past and
present thinkers have talked about rights the same idea or
concept is involved, so that different accounts of this right
represent only different approximations to the truth about
it. Or are they conceptual changes, changes in the ideas
themselves, all of which have been signified by the same
word?

The situation here seems to be like that in which the word
"number" (or its Greek equivalent) has been extended so as
to apply not only to whole numbers but also to irrationals
and, much later, to imaginaries like the square root of minus

one. We calculate with the latter sorts of numbers without loss of our rationality or our grip on reality; and, in doing so, we have managed to pursue our theoretical interests quite effectively. And our talk about rights has played an effective role in our practical affairs, whether rights were conceived as by Locke, still later as by Mill, or as by latter-day thinkers. Recently rights talk has become even more useful as we have come to appreciate that, given the actual and often cruel circumstances of human life, rights must not be viewed only in such general terms that they degenerate into the shibboleths in the service of the privileged that they have often been in the past. Indeed, because some of us have been thinking of rights as the moral property not only of persons but also of at least some of our fellow animals, present-day talk about moral rights has been substantially altered so that increasingly it has done yeoman's work in its service to our moral concerns, just as the greatly expanded and much more sophisticated talk about numbers has enabled us to serve our theoretical interests in ways not imaginable to those Pythagoreans who restricted numbers to those expressible by the ratios of whole numbers.

Have we, then, grasped "the true nature of rights" so that we now see clearly what our predecessors saw only through a glass darkly, that just as we were able to see more clearly the nature of numbers when we saw that we can calculate with numbers like the square roots of two and minus two, so we can see more clearly what a right is when we now employ it as we do in our moral calculations?[1]

Plato, of course, thought that there must be a Form of number, but neither the theory of Forms nor the fact that the same word "number" is used for rationals, irrationals, and imaginaries implies that the same concept of number is involved in all three of these cases. I shall not pursue the

---

1. I shall argue later that the talk about "moral geometry" and "moral calculation" will not do.

analogy with number any further, but ask whether it is possible to arrive at some definitive statement of what a right is—a statement of the necessary and sufficient conditions or features of a right—because rights are employed as indeed they are in our moral thinking. But here a nagging question arises. I have spoken of a right as the moral property of an agent. And we do speak of a right as something that may be claimed, demanded, denied, abridged, waived, transferred, forfeited, respected, relinquished, etc. These very locutions may well be disturbing to some. For they may ask, what is *it*—the right—about which these sorts of things can be said and done? What is the *it* in question? But just as soon as this question is raised, the "it" referred to seems to become more and more mysterious, the more we reflect upon it. This, surely, is the mark of philosophic confusion: that the more we look for something commonplace and familiar, the more it eludes our grasp, so that we are led to appeal to some sort of faculty of intuition in order to explain how it is possible even for those of inferior intelligence to recognize and acknowledge the existence of something each of them and others have, something that plays its characteristic and familiar role in their lives. Let us, therefore, turn to this worry before dealing head on with the question whether or not the accounts of moral rights we have discussed are to be viewed as different attempts to provide a correct or true account of the nature of a right.

In order to lay this worry to rest, along with the threatened philosophical dead end of an appeal to some special moral intuition, we need to ask ourselves how in fact during the course of our moral education we come to understand what it is we are talking about when we talk about rights. Here the answer most certainly is not that we are told that there is some entity called "a right," the properties of which are then brought to our attention by means of examples or description in the way in which we learn the names of various sorts of objects such as "table," "chair," "cat," "dog," etc. Instead, there is a quite homespun way in which we come to understand what a right is. Setting aside the use of this term in which a liberty or privilege is intended, as when a person is said to have a right, within bounds of course, to do as he pleases (i.e., he has a right to sit or stand), we employ, among other things, just those sorts of things to which those who claim to find evidences that the Greeks had some concept of right advert, namely, such facts as that one's bicycle is one's own and not merely that it is in one's physical possession, and that there are some things we owe others when, for example, we borrow what they own. Along with such matters we are given some sort of moral training and education involving such issues as these:

We must not harm those with whom we conduct our affairs.

As Mill put it, we are not "to violate an engagement, either express or implied, or disappoint expectations raised by our own conduct"[2] in word or deed—either by our representations of states of affairs, our assurances, or our explicit promises.

Given that we do care about others with whom we deal, at first our parents, siblings, and friends, and later still others, there are certain commonly understood expectations, connected with these sorts of personal relations, that we must meet, failing which we have given them moral offense or injury even though we may not have injured them physically.

When we misbehave in these cases, we are said to have let others down, to have defeated in these ways the morally legitimate exercise of their agency, and in so doing, to have put ourselves in the position of having to rectify matters in some way: to offer explanations, make amends, suffer remorse, and solicit forgiveness from those one has offended.

Throughout, one learns from the examples afforded by

2. *Utilitarianism*, Chap. V.

one's own conduct and misconduct and that of others. And it is in these ways, among many others in which, as I have put it, the features of rights are exhibited, that one comes to understand that there are rights involved in these cases: that one has acted properly in meeting certain expectations or improperly in letting others down, that is, in failing to give them their due; that the one toward whom one has acted properly or improperly is said to have a right one has either respected or violated; that, to put it in equivalent words, one has met or failed to meet one's obligation to that individual. Instruction is by no means completed once these matters are digested, for one needs to understand what the authority of a right holder is, along with the moral restraints to which that person must submit, even as the person under an obligation to the right holder has the authority of a moral agent in deciding when, if at all, to meet the obligation. And just as explanations are given of what is involved in ascribing rights to siblings, parents, and friends, so explanations are given of the rights of those with whom one has not had any dealings, the casual acquaintance, the stranger, the starving Africans, and those victims of persecution one will never see.

What is imparted to those to whom sorts of explanations are given during the course of their moral education is that the word we use for the moral property of an agent collects together a number of interrelated concepts. When, for example, we explain what is meant by saying that one has waived but not relinquished one's right, we can use quite homely terms in order to fill in the gaps in the understanding of the language of rights. One can say, for example, that what is one's own or what is one's due need not, for certain reasons, on the given occasion, be given to one, without however its ceasing to be what is one's own or one's due. We need not in this instance use the substantival term "right," for the one to whom the explanation is given already has a grasp of some of the features of a right; no vicious circularity is involved in the explanation. And we do not, as Plato supposed we must in his discussion of the relation between the mastery of the sciences and the grasp of the Form of the Good, prepare the way for an ensuing and culminating intuition of a right in the absence of which we would fail "really" to know what we are talking about when we ascribe rights to anyone.

Let us return, now, to the issue, raised earlier, whether or not the correctness of the account of rights to which we have been led consists in its representing the features of some concept more truthfully or accurately than previous accounts. Is it the same concept that past and present thinkers have been concerned to elucidate, or is there a change, for reasons that need to be spelled out, in the very concepts themselves, all of which are designated by the same (or equivalent) substantival word "right"?

If we are to adopt the former alternative, it would appear, given our understanding of what is involved in rights, that one could list a number of the features of rights that constitute the necessary and sufficient condition for their ascription to anyone. If such a set of features could be discovered, one would be compelled to reject forthwith all talk of ascribing rights to animals in some sort of truncated fashion, of speaking of cases in which there is and cases in which there is not any purchase, as I have put it, for the possession of a right. Can such a set of features be found?

It would be absurd to claim that the recognition of a right is essential to its possession, for logically antecedent to the recognition of anything is the existence of what is recognized. It will not do, therefore, to think that where one has no sense of one's right because of one's idyllic marriage, that one has no right against, and no obligation to, one's spouse. So too it is in the case of close friends whose relations are unclouded by any thought either might have that there are moral relations constituted by the rights each has against the other. When things go ideally in relations between those

united by love and affection, there is neither thought nor
mention of the rights and obligations established by their
extensive mutual understandings and expectations; but this
is no reason for denying that there are these moral relations.[3]
Further, slaves who agree with their masters in thinking that
they are a lesser breed of humans are not on that account
devoid of any rights. And so it goes with many other be-
nighted beings as well as with those so immature that they
have no sense of any of their rights.

Far more important is the idea that what is essential to
a right is that it may be asserted and that it may be waived,
relinquished, transferred, or forfeited. Consider, to begin
with, the idea that a right may be asserted. Must this be
done by word? Surely not. The person elbowing his or her
way along the aisle in a crowded bus toward the exit is
asserting a right any passenger has to leave the bus at any
designated stop, without, however, employing any verbal
formula; it may be, in fact, no more rude than the employment of some expression as "I have a right to leave at this
stop" and no less effective in demanding or asserting one's
right.

But however the assertion of one's right may be made, it
does introduce an important consideration that goes beyond
anything involved in the situation in which, as some believe,
the commandments of God, Nature, or Reason are the
ground for all that any moral agent ought to do. Nor is
asserting one's right to be understood as asserting, in the
way in which one does this in providing others with information, that one has some right. For even this statement,
true or false as it may be, is not translatable into the statement that something ought to be done. If it were, the statement that something ought to be done because of a right
that one has would be to make a claim supported by a stut-

---

3. But see Hume, *An Enquiry Concerning the Principles of Morals*, Sec. III,
where he argues that there can be no place for the concept of justice in the relations
between members of a family or close friends.

ter. Asserting one's right is demanding it in one's own name, that is, presenting oneself as one who has the authority to restrict the freedom of others against whom one has the right. This is not the same thing, despite the common confusion on this point by neo-Kantians, as presenting oneself as having the capacity to decide for oneself how to conduct one's affairs on the basis of one's own reason, that is, on the basis of reasons acceptable to all rational creatures. Nor is it the same thing as presenting oneself as some sort of end in itself—whatever that may mean—to whom others must accede if they cherish or "respect" one. To assert one's right is, rather, to exercise a power—to use Locke's term—that is, a moral authority that a right holder has, over the person or persons against whom the former has a right.

It is for this reason that the violation of the right, that is, the failure to meet the correlative obligation, is no mere cause for shame—the moral sentiment appropriate to one who has failed to live up to a commandment imposed upon us all by God or some standard imposed upon one by one's own reason, a standard all rational beings accept—but for guilt, the sense of which is displayed in the distress felt with the realization that one has damaged or eroded another's moral agency. It is for this reason that the victim of this moral damage (or the victim's surrogate, as we noted earlier in our discussion of Locke's view) *and no one else* can forgive the offender. Thus in asserting one's right, one is not merely appealing—if one is appealing at all—to some commonly approved standard of conduct, as we would be if we were to say, for example, that one ought (or ought not) to treat one's spouse in some given way because that form of behavior is prescribed (or proscribed) by one's own reason, or by the requirement that one promote the happiness of mankind or promote the pleasure of sentient creatures or cherish or "respect" some esoteric intrinsic value all of us are supposed to have in common. One is, rather, presenting oneself as a moral agent, who, by virtue of one's status in the particular circumstances in which one finds oneself, can, if need be, bring others to heel in order to preserve one's moral agency. It is this that is missing in those moral theories that take as basic either the notion of a duty to which all of us are subject or the notion of some good to be achieved, as utilitarians of one sort or another would have it, by right action.

The figure of a chain by which one person is bound, the other end of which is held by another, is sometimes employed to represent the moral relation between two persons, the latter being the right holder and the former the person under the correlative obligation. Asserting a right would be represented by having the person holding the end of the chain pull it and thus force the other to move in the right holder's direction. Waiving the right would be represented by the person's holding the end of the chain but providing enough slack in it to allow the other person to have a limited measure of freedom. Relinquishing the right would be shown by the person's releasing his or her hold on the chain. I need not detail the representations of transferring a right or forfeiting it. The figure represents graphically the moral authority of right holders, with respect to which freedom is absolutely essential. It is no accident, therefore, that along with the talk about rights that was introduced in modern times, there was an increased sense of the importance of the freedom of the individual.

What the figure of the chain does *not* convey is the moral requirement imposed upon the right holder to be reasonable in asserting or exercising the right. And although it represents the burden of one who is under an obligation to the right holder, it does not represent the authority that person has, as moral agent, to refuse to meet the obligation in special circumstances, those in which it could be met only at some disproportionately great personal sacrifice.

Let us turn now to the question whether a necessary condition of the possession of any right is that it be assertible.

This, it would appear, is what is implied by those who take the assertibility of rights as one of their central or most important features. The case of infants comes to mind at once. They have rights, although they are incapable of asserting them. For otherwise what would be wrong with killing them, if this could be done painlessly? The fact that their parents would be unhappy? But suppose they are only too happy to be relieved of the burden of raising them? Is it that this sort of thing would, if practiced generally, lead to the extinction of the human race? But in addition to responding with "So much the better" one might consider the case in which the killing of an infant occurs secretly. Is it, then, that the infant would be deprived of the goods it might enjoy if it were allowed to live out its life? But suppose one knew that if it were allowed to live out its life its lot would not in fact be a happy one for itself or for anyone else. Our intuition tells us that even so, it would be immoral to inflict painless death upon it, that even an infant has its rights.

Nor will it do to say it is wrong to kill infants because, although an infant cannot assert its rights, there are others who can function as surrogate for it; for we should not say that it had lost its rights because, unknown to anyone, it had lain in a trash can, or that it had recovered them because someone discovered it and proceeded to care for it. The assertibility of a right no more establishes the fact that there is a right than the fact that the assertibility of a proposition established its truth. If, however, the ground alleged for ascribing rights to infants, who are unable to assert their rights, is that infants are potential adults capable of doing so on their own behalf, the response—assuming that the assertibility of rights is a necessary feature of any right—is surely that this shows, not that infants do have rights, but that they have them only potentially. And, finally, if it is alleged that the case of infants is only a peripheral case in which rights are involved—not a central, full-fledged, or unproblematic sort of case—our response can only be that it is no more problematic to ascribe rights to normal infants than it is to ascribe them to normal adolescents and normal adults. (But more of this later.) Infants do have rights—there is nothing fishy about that—even though they are incapable of asserting them in their own name.

Consider next the question whether a necessary condition—a feature all rights have in common—is that the right can be waived, relinquished, forfeited, or transferred. Here, too, the answer is in the negative, and for the same reason given for the assertibility of rights. Infants have rights but are incapable in principle of engaging in any of these moral performances, not even in the forfeiting of any of their rights. But there is another reason as well. Locke declared that the power to punish those who violate one's rights in the state of nature is transferred to the sovereign with the establishment of civil government; but Locke never claimed that this right to punish offenders against one's rights in the state of nature is, like these latter rights, a natural right. It would in fact have been absurd for him to have done so. For transferring a right, like relinquishing or forfeiting it, is ceasing to have it; but it is impossible to cease to have a natural or human right without ceasing to be a person or moral agent.

Here we need to distinguish between human rights and those special rights that occur only in the case of the special transactions in which moral agents engage, or the special relations in which they stand to others. Friends, for example, cease to have their rights against each other when their friendship is ended. So it is with husband and wife when their ties are severed. In all such cases, moral agents do not cease to be moral agents. We need also to distinguish between special and human rights on the one hand, and, on the other, liberties such as the right to take a walk or purchase a loaf of bread. In the latter cases, the only obligation on the part of others is not to interfere with the exercise of the liberty or right.[4] And we can easily imagine circumstances in which any given liberty may be terminated without compromising the status of the person in question as a moral agent. But it makes no sense to talk about a moral agent's waiving, relinquishing, or forfeiting his or her rights as a moral agent. One can imagine someone's transforming himself into a humanlike creature devoid of any moral sensibilities, as Dr. Jekyll did. But it was not Dr. Jekyll who forfeited his rights as long as he remained Dr. Jekyll, for he was a moral agent. Neither was it Mr. Hyde who forfeited his moral rights, killer though he was; for as Mr. Hyde he was no moral agent and no possessor of any rights. For only a moral agent can waive, relinquish, or forfeit a moral right. But these features of rights—that they can be waived, relinquished, or forfeited—do not apply to human rights and there is no place for them in the case of those too young to have achieved the status of responsible moral agents. Further, it is not only human rights that infants have, but the special right that any infant has against those who have brought it into the world, to receive that special treatment that should be accorded any member of a family and, in the case of any infant, to receive the special attention, care, and affection from the parents that are its due. Here, then, we have a special right any infant has against its parents, a right for which no one else including its parents can function as surrogate in waiving, relinquishing, or forfeiting it.

Someone firmly wedded to the notion that there must be a set of necessary and sufficient conditions for the ascription of rights—for otherwise things are much too untidy, it might

4. But there are cautions. Suppose one has the right to gamble. One can win only if those with whom one plays lose. In a competitive situation the right is to engage in the competition, although that for the sake of which the competition occurs is not something to which one has a right, unless one wins; and in that case others are under an obligation not to interfere with one's taking the money. This is consistent with the fact that in competing as one does against others, one is attempting to prevent them from winning.

seem, for any sort of clear thinking about rights—may retort
by questioning whether unproblematically we can ascribe
rights to infants. The problem remains, however, that there
are borderline cases, cases that are evidences not of unti-
diness in our thinking but of the very nature of our subject
matter. If the infant does not, strictly speaking, have any
rights, at what point in its development does it really have
them? When it is fully mature? But many, if not most, people suffer from arrested moral development. Are we to say,
therefore, that many, if not most, people have no moral
rights at all? In any case the claim that infants have no moral
rights, that they are to be treated as they should be only
because they are objects of our affection, and in the hope
or expectation that they will develop into beings who do
have rights, simply does not ring true. Parents who neglect
their children, at whatever age they may be, forfeit or jeop-
ardize whatever rights parents may have against their offspring, and they do so by failing to meet their obligations
to them. This is to say that their children do have their rights
against them. The courts do allow that children, even infants, have rights, allowing those qualified to do so to function as surrogates for them in defending and exercising their
rights; and there is no good reason to deny that this also
holds in matters of morality.

Elsewhere I have argued that there are reasons for ascribing rights to infants that go beyond the consideration I
have adduced here, and I shall not dwell on them at this
point.[5] Instead, I turn to certain normative features of

5. In my *Rights and Persons*, I argue that it is a mistake to limit our view of
the features of any human being, infant or adult, to those that it has during any
specific part of its life, in determining whether or not to ascribe rights to it during
that time. For example, we do not hesitate to ascribe rights to someone who has
been rendered unconscious by a blow on the head, and not because we believe
that there will be recovery to a normal condition of consciousness. If we did, we
should think ourselves to have been mistaken if the person died without ever re-
gaining consciousness; but we never withdraw our ascription of rights because of
that fact. Whenever we ascribe rights to persons at any given time, whatever their
particular condition at the time may be—drunk or sober, asleep or awake, un-

rights—features mentioned earlier in this essay—in order to show that any attempt to formulate a set of necessary conditions for the ascription of rights is, in principle, altogether misguided.

The features I have in mind might be called desirability (or normative) features. It is desirable, to begin with, that in responding as one should to the person against whom one in fact has a right, one does so not only as a right holder with the authority to demand or assert the right but also as a moral agent who is concerned with the well-being of the person against whom one has the right, and is prepared, therefore, to waive or relinquish the right if it proves excessively burdensome to the other person. And just as the latter must bear whatever burden is involved in the obligation, so that person has the authority as moral agent to refuse to meet the obligation if quite unforeseeable circumstances have arisen that will prove to be disastrous to the right holder. But this surely implies that both the right holder and the person under the correlative obligation are concerned with each other's well-being. In this world, however, people are not as caring about each other as they should be, even when they are bound by the moral relations constituted by their rights and obligations. Some misconstrue the conscientiousness with which they regard the moral relations in which they stand to others as a necessity that is indifferent to and altogether independent of any feelings of

---

conscious or not—we view those particular periods of the lives of persons within the broader context of their active, waking, and responsible lives. And in thinking of an infant as having its rights, we think of it as a human being at the very earliest phase of life in which development and maturation, by virtue of its native endowments, and with proper nurture, take place over a considerable period of time. It is because of this broader conception of what is involved in the life of a human being, rather than a tunnel vision view of the features exhibited by an infant, that we ascribe rights to it, just as we do in the case of someone who is unconscious. An infant that dies in infancy is deprived of a life in which, given normal conditions of nurture, it would have been able at a later stage to assert its rights, and, where appropriate, to waive, relinquish, or forfeit them. It is because we have this normal and natural development in mind that we think of an infant as *a person in its infancy* and, therefore, ascribe rights to it.

affection for or concern about the well-being of others.[6] For these people, a promise, for example, is a promise, to be kept no matter what, as if it were made in the sight of the Lord, to be kept at all costs. And, whatever duties the members of a family have for each other, these are to be performed, they think, if need be without any trace of the mutual concern and affection each may have for the others. But such Gothic attitudes, undesirable as they are, are no grounds for denying that those who exhibit warm feeling towards each other do stand in moral relations constituted by their rights and obligations.

Similarly, there are those who are less than admirable in the ways in which they violate the rights of others, and who suffer no remorse for their misdeeds. So, too, are those who are unforgiving toward others who have abridged or violated their rights and who demonstrate not mere regret but the pangs of guilt and remorse. There are those who recognize that they have behaved badly toward others but appear indifferent to the necessity of offering explanations or making amends for their offense. To mention only one more kind of moral inadequacy, there are those who are scrupulous in the way in which they meet their obligations toward the members of their own small in-group but appear to be altogether indifferent to the moral relations in which they stand to outsiders.

None of the sorts of persons I have described need be psychopaths; they are, far more often than not, moral agents who in one respect or another and to a greater or less degree are morally flawed. The rights (and obligations) they do in fact have are central cases; but their conception of the role

6. In this connection, consider H. A. Prichard's sharp distinction between duty and virtue in "Does Moral Philosophy Rest on a Mistake?" (in his posthumously published collection, *Moral Obligation* [Oxford: Oxford University Press, 1949]), along with Mill's conception of so-called duties of perfect obligation, from which the so-called duties of imperfect obligation, e.g., the duty that we are to be concerned with the well-being of others, appear to be distinguished as independent moral considerations.

that rights should play in the lives of moral agents differs from our conception, to which the whole panoply of concepts involved in our understanding of rights applies. It is not merely that as *we* see it, the persons I have described accept but fail to live up to the standards provided by what I have called the desirability features of rights, and hence that their deficiencies lie merely in their performances rather than in their conceptions of their rights and obligations. It is, rather, that as *we* see it, their moral development has been arrested and that, along with this, their moral notions are relatively impoverished, that is, defective. For we can imagine moral codes with respect to which what *we* should regard as imperfections in moral thinking are regarded by those who subscribe to the codes as altogether satisfactory. And this implies that the very concepts embodied in such moral codes are different from those which *we* employ in our moral thinking, in consequence of which our panoply of notions, including desirability features, is involved in their conception of a right at best only in a truncated form.

We have seen, first, that the features of special moral rights differ from those of human rights; second, that in the case of infants some of the features of the rights of moral agents are absent; and, third, that the desirability features of rights are reflected in different ways in various conceptions of rights. The conclusion to be drawn from all of this is that there is no single conception of moral rights with respect to which different so-called theories approximate to a greater or lesser degree the correct analysis of rights. What we have, in short, is not a single concept of moral rights. For the term "right" is a cluster term, one that brings together a number of different features of rights that vary with the types of rights, the maturation of right holders, and with what we should like to call their moral enlightenment.

8. Moral Progress

The idea of progress involves the idea of some movement toward some desired end. Although one can speak of the progress a maniacal murderer is making toward freedom as he is loosening his bonds, generally what we have in mind when we speak of progress is the idea of some end that is not only desired but desirable. It is understandable, therefore, that when we speak of moral progress or progress in our moral thinking, what we have in mind is some ideal state of affairs toward which some movement has been or is being made. If utilitarians are correct, the question whether any moral progress has been made since antiquity would be answered by determining whether or not there has been an increase in the general happiness. How, of course, this is to be understood is another matter, for we can understand quite a number of different things that might be meant by "the general happiness." Does it mean the total happiness without regard to the amount of unhappiness, the total net balance of happiness over unhappiness, the average of either of these, or something else? Further, is the ideal to which the utilitarian is committed the condition in which all persons without exception, perhaps even all sentient creatures, are wholly free of any pain or unpleasantness and in an uninterrupted and most intense state of euphoria? And anti-utilitarians, conspicuously Plato, not infrequently have set forth in some detail their own conceptions of the morally ideal states of affairs in terms of which the notion of moral progress is to be fully spelled out.

In our initial review of some of the most important treatments of moral rights since first mention of them was made, we seemed to find some sort of progressive development of ideas, from Occam, to Locke, to Mill, and, finally, to those who in quite recent days have spoken out in support of human and even animal rights. Although it would be a mistake to suppose that the thinking about rights to which we have been led represents a correct and hence better analysis of the concept of a moral right than those offered by our predecessors, it does seem that our way of thinking about rights—our concept of a moral right—is better, morally more enlightened. And if this is so, surely those who employ this way of thinking about rights and fashion their conduct in accordance with the normative demands these impose upon them, conduct themselves in ways that represent some progress from our present uneven, indeed sorry state. In that case, it would appear, there is some morally ideal state of affairs that could be delineated.

But in the preceding chapter, in the picture presented of the ways in which fully responsible agents conduct themselves, blamelessly, in situations in which they must make moral choices, the situations described are surely less than ideal. It is not an ideal state of affairs when an agent must choose between keeping some relatively trivial promise and saving the life of one's friend, even though no moral problem is involved in this case. No moral theory could reasonably be expected to solve every moral problem in business, medicine, and engineering or in our everyday relations with each other, in such a fashion that no injury of any sort remains, and no compunction need be felt because of the denial of a right. Still less should we expect a moral theory to resolve to the satisfaction of everyone concerned every possible moral dilemma that might conceivably arise. For example, we should indeed condemn someone who without any compunction betrayed his country in order to save a close friend; but equally we should consider his action to be less than ideal if he did it in anguish, realizing its consequences for his country and his countrymen.

Plato, after raising the question "What is justice?" proceeds on a search for the nature of justice in its ideal condition and, after much reflection, announces that it consists, in the case of the individual, in a smoothly functioning soul free from any of the remorse and distress occasioned by any choices that moral agents are required to make. Small wonder, then, that in giving the nod to the just man in response to Thrasymachus' question, he simply takes it for granted, without any sense of the necessity of looking to the actual cases in which moral agents are involved, that truth telling and promise keeping—to mention only two of the many cases in which rights and their correlative obligations are involved—will contribute invariably to the happiness of the agent.

II

Plato assumes, of course, that in matters of morals it is possible to achieve knowledge of the kind that science, in principle, can provide. And here I want to examine briefly one small feature of Plato's dream of an ideal world in which science provides us, albeit in a very limited way, with a certain model for moral understanding. What I have in mind is the recent version of the attempt to pattern principles after scientific principles in D. W. Ross's discussion of moral principles so-called, for example, that one ought to tell the truth, keep one's promises, preserve human life, and so on.[1]

Ross is clear enough that while such so-called principles can conflict, there is no reason to reject any of them. In science, a conflict of principles is a certain indication that something is amiss, that one of the principles needs to be

1. *The Right and the Good* (Oxford: Oxford University Press, 1930), Chap. II.

abandoned, at least in the form in which it is stated. How then are we to preserve the analogy between scientific and moral principles without abandoning what seems essential to both sorts of cases, namely, that a principle, of whichever kind, is a universally quantified proposition? Ross's answer is twofold: (a) the laws of nature in physics should be understood as universally quantified propositions about the tendencies that exist in physical phenomena, for example, the tendencies of gases to behave in the ways specified by the laws of gases, and (b) the principles of morality so-called, for example, that one ought to keep one's promises, are to be understood as universally quantified propositions about the tendencies of certain kinds of moral actions to be right in the sense that those particular actions in those particular situations are morally required.

No doubt the vast majority of promise-keeping acts are right—the refusal or failure to keep one's promise is the correct course of action in exceptional cases only—hence Ross writes about the tendency of promise-keeping actions to be right. But this good common sense is obscured by the philosophical move he makes in his representation of the import of this tendency of certain sorts of actions. For now we are to understand the statement that one ought to keep one's promises as the universally quantified statement that promise-keeping acts are tending-to-be-right actions, just as we are to understand a statement about the inverse relation between temperature and pressure of a gas, given that the volume remains constant, as a universally quantified statement of the tendency for all gases to maintain an inverse relation between temperature and pressure. The result of this move in the case of the laws of gases is the denial of the invariance commonly understood as essential to causal relations. The result in the moral case is the introduction of a new kind of "ought," "duty," "right," and "obligation," which one might label, respectively, as "tending-to-be-right," and "tending-to-be-obligation"; and these Ross and his followers now label "*prima facie* ought." "*prima facie* duty," "*prima facie* right," and "*prima facie* obligation," respectively.

Consider now the so-called prima facie obligation to keep a promise. The obligation, Ross tells us, is genuine or objective, not merely apparent; for it remains to be reckoned with even when, justifiably, the obligation is not met. And in saying that a prima facie obligation is a different kind of obligation from an obligation *sans* qualification, Ross is saying that this difference is quite different from the difference that exists between, for example, the obligation to keep a promise and the obligation to save the life of a human being. For to say that an obligation is a prima facie obligation is *not* to say that one is morally required to meet it. To say that it is an obligation *simpliciter* or an obligation *sans* qualification is to say that not meeting the obligation would be wrong, period. If one supposed, therefore, that "one ought to keep promises" meant that in every case in which there is an obligation incurred by a promise and there is an opportunity to meet the obligation, it would be reprehensible not to do so, one would subscribe to the moral absurdity that every promise is to be kept no matter what the circumstances may be. In order to avoid this way of construing the alleged generality of the "principle" that promises ought to be kept, the "ought" (and so, too, with the "obligation" in the statement that one is under an obligation to keep a promise) is now said to be only prima facie.

The view is paradoxical. Words like "ought," "obligation," and "duty" are said to be used in one sense when they are employed in statements of moral principles and in a different sense when they are used in sentences expressing an agent's decision about what he is to do in a specific situation to which the moral principle applies. This would be like saying, assuming that there is an analogy between moral and physical principles, that in the statement of the laws of gases, "pressure" means one thing, and in the statement of the conclusion drawn about the pressure of some gas in some specific situation, it means something else.

But if we reject this talk about different senses, how can one account for the generality in a statement like "one ought to keep promises" while preserving the characteristic use of sentences to express one's conclusion about what one must do in some given situation? Not by seizing upon the fact that "I ought to keep my promise" is about *this* particular person, whereas "one ought to keep promises" is about anyone: for this generality is also involved in the use of "I ought to keep my promises, but . . ." (and here one goes on to state what the special, excusing circumstances of this case are). The generality is to be found, rather, in what is implied by anything's being a moral reason, namely, its essential generality. If x is a reason for doing y, then it is a reason for doing anything to which it is a relevant consideration. Certainly Ross and Prichard, among other intuitionists of the past, were correct in thinking that the statement that promises ought to be kept is self-evident; for one would reveal that one did not understand the notion of a promise if one were to deny that promises are to be kept. But any promise-keeping act is and must be something more than just a promise-keeping act; for it is a promise-keeping act only if, for example, it is the payment of a sum of money, the help given to paint a house or to care for someone's mother, or anything else that one has promised to do. Hence, in considering what one must do in a given situation on which the promise has a bearing, one is considering more than the self-evident "one ought to keep promises." One is considering also whether the fact that one has promised and, therefore, that one has a good moral reason for doing the promise-keeping act, whatever that act may be, is sufficient reason in that situation, then and there, for doing it. The so-called moral principle serves, therefore, to call attention to, or to remind one of, the fact that there is a reason for doing some specific act, namely, that to do it would be to keep a promise.

Instead of speaking of "tending-to-be-oughts" rather than "oughts" that specify "oughts *simpliciter*," we should speak of the fact that the moral reason specified by some moral precept or maxim may or may not be sufficient to determine what it is that one ought to do in some specific case to which it applies. But since, in the vast majority of such cases, the reason is sufficient, conflicts of rights and obligations, for example, are the exception rather than the rule. It is this fact that lies behind, but is obscured by, Ross's talk about the tendencies of "oughts." It is this fact that is obscured by Ross's use of the expression "prima facie"; for it may only be apparent, something that at first sight appears to be the case, that in some exceptional cases the reasons conveyed by the use of sentences like "one ought to keep one's promises," which normally play decisive roles in justifying certain particular acts, do not do so at all. If different uses are to be distinguished in moral discourse, it is not in the uses of words like "ought," "duty," or "right." It is, rather, that the use of sentences like, for example, "one ought to keep one's promises," which play their role in communication and reflection in the manner I have just described, is different from the use of sentences "I ought to keep my promise" to express, for example, decisions about what is to be done in specific cases, failing which there is moral wrongdoing.

We need not tarry long over the current talk about so-called prima facie rights. The idea here is that a right is said to be prima facie if every right-exercising or right-according act is prima facie right, this last term being understood in some such way as Ross described in his talk about prima facie duties and obligations. Here again the effort is designed to preserve the generality of the thesis that one ought to provide or allow right holders with that to which they have rights, and the points made above in our review of the talk about so-called prima facie oughts, obligations, and duties apply here as well. But it is worth asking what it is with which prima facie rights are to be contrasted. Is it a right *simpliciter*, something that a prima facie right becomes when it serves in a particular situation as a decisive reason for performing the right-exercising or right-according act? Are we to say that what had been one kind of right becomes, in that particular situation, a different kind of right? That, surely, is to conflate two very different matters, namely, the fact that there *is* a right with the fact that the right plays a role in the justification of conduct. Or, given that it is sometimes said that such and such a right is only a prima facie right, are prima facie rights to be contrasted with rights in that popular and absurd sense of the term that even Locke, despite the obscurities of his treatment of rights, does explicitly reject, namely, absolute rights? So that by saying that *A* has an absolute right to *x*, one implies that *A* is fully justified in demanding *x* whenever he wishes to do so? But I should like to say about the allegedly sacred or 'absolute' right to life that any human being is sometimes said to have, that if I had to choose between taking the life of a Hitler and betraying my friend, I hope I would not hesitate to put an end to the life of that moral monster.

The talk about prima facie rights, duties, obligations, oughts, etc., is the last-gasp attempt to preserve the notion that moral principles or precepts—call them what you wish—are universally quantified propositions about what ought to be done. It is high time we gave it the interment it deserves.

III

Let us now return to the question raised earlier, whether the idea of moral progress involves some idea of a morally ideal state of affairs. Progress, it seems plausible enough to suppose, consists in movement toward an end. What can this be if it is not some best possible state of affairs for moral agents? But if we ask what that state of affairs can possibly be, the answer is by no means obvious. For even if all conflicts of obligation were resolved in the best possible manner, some would of necessity give way to others; and the fact that someone's right is infringed, for good and sufficient reasons, is not, it would appear, the best possible state of affairs. Certainly it is far from the best of possible circumstances if anyone were faced with the dilemma of choosing between betraying one's friend and betraying one's country. But it is also not the best of all possible states of affairs if one must choose between keeping an engagement with a student who wants to chat and taking one's child on a promised trip to the zoo. Nor does every conflict between the interests of different persons pose a moral issue. If *A* competes with *B* for a prize, the issue is not a moral one, unless, of course, there is some question of fairness about the competition, but one of superiority in the particular sort of performance. But as long as the interests of different individuals compete for satisfaction, there is the *possibility* of moral conflict given the mutual understandings and expectations that may occur. And when there are such conflicts the situations are less than ideal. The question that needs to be asked is whether it is possible to imagine a world in which no choices between rights, or, for that matter, between moral considerations of any sort could ever arise?

Hume, during the course of his discussion of justice, asks us to imagine a "*poetical* fiction of the *golden age*" in which, among other possibilities, there is such an improvement in the character of human beings that "every man has the utmost tenderness for every man, and feels no more concern for his own interest than for that of his fellows."[2] "Why should I bind another, by a deed or promise, to do me any

---

2. *An Enquiry Concerning the Principle of Morals*, Sec. III, Pt. I; italics are Hume's.

good office," he asks, "when I know that he is already prompted, by the strongest inclination, to seek my happiness, and would, of himself, perform the desired service . . . ?" He goes on to remark, interestingly enough, that "[e]very man, upon this supposition, being a second self to another, would trust all his interests to the discretion of every man."[3] Hume takes this to be like the case in which "the whole human race would form only one family," but it is by no means clear that this is quite the same thing as the supposition that each person would be "a second self to another." For what are we asked to imagine in this "poetical fiction"? That people are much more warmly disposed to each other, so that each stands ready, far more frequently than is now the case, to help others get what they want? Or is this what is being presented: the picture of each person's wanting *only* to have others get what they want? Certainly we can imagine without any difficulty or incoherence that the human race is one big happy family, whose members are far more disposed than they are in actual fact to help one another. But this is not the same thing as each one's being "a second self to another" so that no possibility of conflict of interest could ever arise. For in a family whose members are very close to one another, who have, as we say, common interests, the fact that they do have interests in common does not preclude the possibility of any conflict. If A has the same interest as B in x and the same interest as B in y, A may want x when B wants y in circumstances in which the pursuits of these interests conflict. A is interested in music, as is B, and in studying medicine, as is B; but A cannot turn on the phonograph in the room they share without distracting B from his studies.

Or, to avoid any possible conflict in interests that conceivably could give rise to a conflict or rights, are we to imagine that A wants whatever B wants whenever B wants

3. Ibid.

it and that *B* wants whatever *A* wants whenever *A* wants
it? And generalizing from these two individuals, whoever
they may be, to all others without exception—for how else
could one preclude all possibility of moral conflict—are we
now to imagine such a "harmony" between all individuals
as would obliterate the distinction between individuals—
young and old, male and female, and so on indefinitely—
so that the distinction between any two persons disappears
and all persons collapse into one? How else, indeed, could
"every man . . . [be] a second self to another"? Or are we
to imagine that the "poetical fiction" is the "fiction" that
the only thing each person wants is that everyone else get
what he or she wants? A fiction, however, is some conceiv-
able state of affairs; so does it make sense to speak about
a wanting that consists simply in wanting whatever anyone
else wants? For what, one needs to know, does anyone
want? The "fiction" is as incomprehensible as the picture
presented on one interpretation of the Leibnizian doctrine
that the state of each monad consists simply in the mirroring
of the states of other monads, namely, the mirroring of the
mirroring of the mirroring . . . What is being mirrored by
any monad? So, too, in the case of the fiction that the only
thing that anyone wants is that everyone get what he or she
wants. It must be possible to give descriptions of what is
wanted, independently of the fact that others want these
wants to be satisfied, if the description of the "fiction" is to
make any sense, just as some description of the states of the
monads, apart from the fact that they mirror each other, is
needed if we are to make any sense of the Leibnizian mon-
adology. But if we are given any independent description of
the wantings, we are back once more to the possibility of
conflicts between the wantings of different persons. In order
to avoid this possibility, the distinction between persons
must collapse, each being "a second self of another," in
which case it makes no sense to speak about any moral

relations between persons—their rights and their correlative
obligations—for all persons have now become one.

The upshot of the argument is that if moral progress involves the conception of some ideal, this cannot be any imaginable state of affairs in which all possible conflicts of
rights and obligations have disappeared. Moral burdens cannot be *morally* undesirable, however difficult, unpleasant,
inconvenient, or in any other respect undesirable they may
happen to be. But this should not surprise us, given the fact
that morality *can* be a demanding mistress. The Platonic
ideal of justice, in which everything goes harmoniously and
happily, untouched by burdens, discomforts, regrets, and
even the pangs of guilt that are inescapable aspects of the
moral life, is nothing less than philosopher's nonsense.

IV

If we have made progress in our thinking about rights in
the ways described in this essay, this is not progress in the
analysis of "the concept of a right." What has developed,
as we have seen during the course of our discussion, is the
sequence of accounts that have been proposed over the centuries—a sequence to which I hope this essay contributes—
of the ways we *should* think of rights. And this implies that
the revised ways in which we are to think of rights and
obligations are progressively better in the sense that, if we
were to think of rights in the ways recommended and if we
were to conform to the normative requirements they impose
on our thought and action, there would be moral progress.
But the progress in question cannot be, for reasons that
should now be clear enough, a closer approximation to some
ideal in which all moral issues are happily resolved and no
burdens, regrets, or sense of guilt remain—a state from
which these characteristic features of the moral life have simply disappeared. Instead, progress is toward a condition of

our lives that remains characteristically moral yet is superior to what has been envisaged by those before us who have recognized the importance of rights.

Instead of looking for some optimal state of affairs in which goods have been maximized and evils have been eliminated, we should look at the nature of a moral community and an optimal state of the moral relations among its members as the moral ideal in terms of which moral progress is to be understood. The members of the moral community are moral agents—human or otherwise—who are, or should be, prepared to establish those mutual understandings that enable them to support one another's activities, or to refrain from interfering with these—so that they may pursue their separate or concerted interests successfully, achieving for themselves, or for others, the goods these interests define. Conspicuously, this is true of those who engage in paradigmatic promise-transactions. But it is also true of the members of a family that is as it should be, of friends, of acquaintances, and even of those who are complete strangers, who, for example, assume without any reflection and simply as a matter of course that they will not harm one another during their chance encounters in public places. And if there is any reason to think that some animals have rights, it should be true of them that they are prepared to enter into understandings with us, as indeed we should be with them— understandings, at the very least, not to interfere or engage in violent behavior.

In this brief sketch we have underscored the fact that the members of the moral community are not individuals who go about their affairs independently of and with indifference toward one another. Each is disposed to stand in moral relations to the other, prepared to engage in ties that bind them together as they go about their affairs. Each, of course, is an individual in the commonplace sense that he or she has a distinctive personality, a set of personality traits, interests, abilities, hopes, and aspirations; but each is also a social being as a member of the moral community with a life that is in important respects joined with those of others. It is not only that we need one another in order to obtain goods no one can procure unaided; it is also that we are concerned about others, even the total stranger, and are prepared, if we live up to the normative requirements imposed upon us by our membership in the moral community, to care for each other if need be. For as moral agents, the members of the moral community have rights, if for no other reason than that they *are* moral agents. And although we can easily understand why many can be indifferent, in our own society, to the fundamental rights of the homeless and the undernourished, this only goes to show how far the normative requirements of membership in the moral community are not being met. We are our brothers' keepers, whether or not we recognize it. We owe others the help we can give them without which they cannot live lives worth living; their title to this help is simply the fact that they are moral agents.

V

Let us now turn to a consideration of the main deficiencies of the views of those in the past who recognized the importance of moral rights.

1. As we saw earlier, it would be a mistake to suppose that, on Locke's view, men are egoistic and indifferent to the well-being of their fellows.[4] Recall that he quotes with approval the words of "the judicious Hooker" that "we are naturally induced to seek communion and fellowship with others." The reasons given for the "natural duty" we have to love others, to assist them, and to preserve their lives are "the natural equality of men," the desire that each has for the "love and affection" of others, the assistance that others can

4. See Chap. 2, Sec. II, above.

give one in the acquisition of goods, and the moral requirement applicable to each man to preserve his own life.[5] How
this *de facto* insufficiency of each to make do without the
help of others in securing the goods we desire, including the
affections of others and the security each has in his own life,
can entail that there are the moral obligations on the part
of each to provide the necessary goods, affection, and the
security in the lives of others, Locke makes no attempt to
explain. It is "the law of nature . . . and reason, which is
that law"[6]—however *that* is to be understood—which is designed to fill the conceptual gap. The law of nature (reason—or whatever it is that it reveals) exercises its jurisdic-
tion over individuals and ensures the moral requirement that
each person is to make up for our natural insufficiencies in
goods, affection, and security in our lives. But when Locke,
in his account of "person" in his *Essay Concerning Human
Understanding*, writes that it is "a forensic term, appropri-
ating actions and their merit; and so belongs only to *intelligent agents*, capable of a law,"[7] he is saying that what
binds each of us to others is a law to which all are equally
subject, not something about each one of us that constitutes
our social nature and in this way links each person with
everyone else.

All this is a far cry from the conception of a person as
an inherently social being, whose nature cannot be understood independently of the relations in which it stands to
others. It fails to do justice to our conviction that human
beings, as moral agents or persons, are bound to each other
in ways that enable them to join their lives and deal with
each other, minimally as human beings, but also as friends,
siblings, promisors and promisees, etc. It fails to recognize
that persons *care* about one another not because of the requirement of some law from on high to which they are sub-

5. *Second Treatise*, para. 5.
6. Ibid., para. 6.
7. Bk. II, Chap. XXVII, sec. 26.

ject but because of their nature as social beings, without which they could not enter into those mutual understandings by virtue of which they stand ready as circumstances require to assist one another in their endeavors. If it is objected that there are psychopaths and sociopaths who are devoid of any degree of concern for other members of the species Homo sapiens, this only points to the unsurprising fact that "human being" and "person" as we employ these terms in our common discourse during the course of our familiar activities are not, like "Homo sapiens," terms of biology.

Hume thought that we could account for the fellow-feeling we have for any other person by means of the mechanism of sympathy by means of which the mere recognition of the pleasures and pains of others is transformed into sympathetic pleasures and pains of our own. Sympathetic pleasures and pains, however, are hardly sufficient to explain the closeness for our attachments to the members of our families or to our close friends. And they are much too diffuse to explain our concern about starving people in distant lands; Hume's attempt to invoke his mechanism of sympathy so that the mere mental picture of such starving persons in remote places is transformed into a passion is testimony to his ingenuity but not to his understanding of the conceptual features, or grammar, of the terms he invokes in his account. Indeed, the sympathy one feels for someone who is crying out in pain in one's full view is hardly enough to establish that one does in fact care for the sufferer.

Consider, for example, the executioner who goes about his grisly tasks—"A job is, after all, a job, and one must live"—as a matter of course, steeling himself against his victims' suffering by diverting his attention with pleasant thoughts as he does what he thinks he must do. Does the fact that he must divert attention from his victims as much as possible and perform his duties mechanically, as it were, without thinking about what he is doing, show that he cares about them? Hardly; there are, after all, people who are

crafty in their ability to divert their attention from the havoc
they create, but whom we should never describe as loving
or caring. Consider, too, the familiar case of the motorist
who hurriedly drives past the scene of an accident in order
to avoid the intensification of his own feelings of discomfort
that stopping to help the injured would cause; he is uncom-
fortable because of what he has seen—but he could say to
himself, "After all, the feeling will go away." Does he care
about the victims of the accident? So far, the answer cannot
be that he does. Suppose, however, that he is remorseful and
a few moments later returns to render assistance to the injured. Now the situation has changed; he really does care.
Of course, one would not say that a person is caring if he
remains untroubled about the suffering of anyone else; but
saying that someone cares is no mere report about sympathetic feelings. Whatever else it is, it is also saying something
about someone's character: that the person is disposed to
help those in need simply because they need it.

What, then, is characteristic of the members of the moral
community? Not that equality of human beings that Locke,
following Hooker, supposes—that is, the equal desire they
have for goods, including the affection of others—an equality on the basis of which the "law of nature . . . and reason,
which is that law" requires each of us to return affection
for affection received. For each of us might desire the affection of others without having the slightest disposition to
return it. Rather, what characterizes the members of the
moral community is the fact that they are, by their own
nature as the moral agents they are, disposed to care about
and, as circumstances warrant, to care for others.

2. It is frequently supposed that any conception of moral
rights commits one to some sort of individualism. What is
meant by "individualism" is by no means clear. For reasons
stated earlier, Locke's "individualism" cannot be taken to
be an egoistic conception of human beings. Presumably what

is intended is a view that is opposed to what might be described as a social conception of human beings, but how this is to be understood is usually left unspecified by those who describe Locke's view as individualistic. I shall not attempt to provide a general account or definition of what is or should be meant by "individualism." I shall, instead spell out some of the salient features of Locke's view which have led to the application of the label "individualism" to his doctrine, in order to contrast it with the features of the conception of moral rights advanced in this essay.

Locke tells us that "every man has a property in his own person" to which "nobody has any right . . . but himself." Here "property" is being used by Locke not only to include external possessions but also liberty and even life itself.[8] In his account of the acquisition of property by clearing the land in a wilderness that God has given all men in common, Locke tells us that by mixing with the land the labor of one's body, which is properly one's own, one makes the result one's own, that is, a part of oneself, and hence something in which one has a property right. It is unnecessary here to review the familiar objections that have been raised against this account.[9] What is important here is the idea that in possessing or acquiring property rights—broadly or narrowly conceived—that to which one has or acquires a right becomes part of one's person or turf, to be protected precisely because it is one's own. How Locke would explain the right conferred by a promise we do not know; and given the scandalously unsatisfactory treatment of the topic in his own time, it is perhaps well that he made no attempt to do so. It would have been patently absurd for him to declare that when a promise is made, there occurs a mutually advantageous exchange of benefits and burdens such that what is promised becomes part of the promisee's person just as,

8. On these points see *Second Treatise*, paras. 27 and 123.
9. Some of these are reviewed in my *Rights and Persons*, pp. 229–230.

when one mixes one's labor with the land one clears in the wilderness, the result becomes part of one's person and, therefore, something in which one has a property right. In any case, the explanation Locke offers of the right of everyone in the state of nature to punish any offender against anyone does not employ this model; for this right is one in the absence of which, he declares, no one would be secure in one's property right. However Locke does or would explain rights other than his fundamental rights, the latter are to be understood as rights to one's own person, or turf, to be protected from incursion or violation by others.

Locke's conception of our fundamental rights is thus protectionist in character. It is with a view to the protection of these rights in the state of nature that everyone in that state must come to the assistance of those whose lives, liberties, and goods are threatened. It is with a view to the protection of rights in that state, by deterring people from invading the rights of others, that everyone has a right to punish transgressors. And it is with a view to protecting their rights that persons accept the authority of a sovereign, an authority the latter may exercise only to the extent provided by the terms of the covenant. In short, fundamental or natural rights are invoked by Locke in order to justify the protection of one's own turf.

On Locke's view, there is no intimation of any right the starving, the poor, and the homeless may have against those who are capable of relieving them of their distress. Indeed, despite the talk about a natural duty to love others, there is no sense of any duty to help the impoverished. For, as Locke and his well-to-do contemporaries saw it, the world provides ample opportunities for the acquisition of the goods necessary for anyone's well-being; and, if they took any notice of those in rags, their unsavory appearance only served to reinforce the conviction that poverty is the result of indolence or vice. We know better, of course; hence our talk about human rights—the rights any human being has as a moral agent—and of what we owe the victims of circumstances over which they have no control: the poverty they endure because of the accidents of their birth, social and economic circumstances, and lack of education, not to mention the various accidents of nature.

We ought to do what we can to remove the distress of these victims of circumstance, whoever they may be, not out of kindness, or a desire to add to the general happiness of mankind, as utilitarians would have it, but because of the moral relation in which we stand to any moral agent merely because of the agent's membership with us in the moral community. As agents in a moral community, persons are not only the possessors of property—their lives, liberties, and the goods they have acquired—but agents who pursue or ought to pursue interests of which they are capable and by which they may achieve, for themselves and for others, the goods these define. And as members of the moral community they will, if they meet the normative requirements of their membership, care about and if need be—given that they are capable of doing so without needless and unwarranted sacrifice—care for those who suffer the various forms of deprivation that blight their lives. In short, the rights that persons have as moral agents must not be narrowly conceived as pertaining to their property but broadly conceived as reflecting their status as members of the moral community. It is for this reason that the impoverished have rights against us, that we can meet our obligations to them not by protecting them in the security of their right to property— for there is nothing there to be protected from trespass— but by providing them, as far as we are able, with what they need in order to live lives worth living.

Many or most of us recognize now not only our responsibility to help the disadvantaged but also the incorrectness of previous views of the extent of membership in the moral community. Earlier we discussed the question whether some animals have moral rights; if they do, they will have to be included as members of the moral community. In that case we shall have to speak not of human rights but of the fundamental rights of any moral agent. To what extent this widening of the membership of the moral community may be justified, only further empirical studies can determine.

But there are other matters to which attention needs to be directed. We know now a good deal more than our forebears did about the nature and extent of mental disease, in consequence of which we now recognize that many cases of what had appeared to be moral culpability are really cases of mental incapacity. In the courts, the plea of not guilty by reason of insanity may often serve as a dodge in order to avoid punishment; but it is also fully warranted in some of the cases brought to trial. A man who kills another for gain is punishable for his offense; but let the number of the killings be increased a thousandfold and we have more than a mere suspicion that our killer is really insane. We know now that many of those wandering about in the streets, homeless and sometimes eating food from garbage containers, are suffering from mental illness (others, of course, are not and need a helping hand in order to regain their position in the mainstream of society). While these need food and shelter, they also need to be treated not as moral agents but as patients in mental hospitals. Here again we need to know more about the morally incapacitating mental diseases of many who live on the fringes of society, wandering about in the streets or protected in private homes and hospitals. And here, too, there are borderline cases in which there can be no simple "Yes" or "No" answer to the question whether these are moral agents who can be held responsible for their conduct and who have moral rights, the alternative being to put them away in hospitals for treatment and dealt with as humanely as possible. Rather, we need to deal with these cases in ways that are appropriate to their quite specific conditions and with suitable care and caution. Nature does not cater to our desire for a set of neatly divided cubby-holes into which anything that comes along can be properly put.

3. Mill, sensible as he was about some important features of moral rights and liberal as he was in his views on a number of social issues, such as freedom of speech and the liberation of women, exhibits a seriously misshapen individualism in his own theory of moral rights. Here, as with Locke, there is the failure to recognize the fact that persons, as moral agents, are members of the moral community and that because they are subject to the normative requirements of such membership, they must view their moral rights and the role rights play in their lives in the light of these requirements. Recall Mill's endorsement of the traditional distinction between duties of perfect obligation and those of imperfect obligation. The latter requires, among other things, that each of us be concerned with the well-being of others. But since this requirement is independent of any duty of perfect obligation precisely because quite different rules are involved, the requirement imposed upon persons in promise transactions are independent of any rule pertaining to concern with the well-being of others. The goodness of virtuous action and that of promise keeping are, as Prichard later put it, "co-ordinate and independent."[10] A duty of perfect obligation may be exacted from one, Mill tells us, as one may exact a debt. Why then make or keep promises? Because they are eminently useful. Keeping a promise is providing a good for the promisee; and one enters into promise transactions because it involves an eminently useful exchange of benefits and burdens to both of the parties concerned.

It is unnecessary to repeat the objections to this view stated in our critical examination of Mill's account in chap-

10. "Does Moral Philosophy Rest on a Mistake?" p. 12n.

ter 4 above. First-, second-, and third-person promises all bind, even when there is no useful exchange of benefits and burdens, and even when the benefits provided by the promise-keeping acts are to persons other than the promisees. And, as the numerous examples cited during our examination of Mill's view show, considerations of the well-being of a right holder, or of the person under the correlative obligation, are good reasons that may well be sufficient for waiving and even relinquishing the right or for refusing to meet the obligation. This should not be surprising in view of the fact that right holders and those bound to them are moral agents who are members of the moral community and *as such* are subject to the normative requirement to care about and, when the need and opportunity to do so arises, to care for others.

That we are social beings who, as members in good standing in the moral community, do care about one another is shown by our willingness as moral agents, that is, as those who have the fundamental rights of all such agents, to enter into the mutual understandings by which we support one another's agency. This willingness in fact is one of the criteria we do employ in deciding whether any agent is a being endowed with rights. Agents may have desires and interests; but unless they exhibit some measure of willingness to enter into mutual understandings by which they will support our agency as we support theirs, we are well advised not to ascribe moral rights to them. But if this be granted, it is evident that persons, as moral agents, are by their very nature social beings; for they are concerned with one another's well-being, and disposed not to go it alone in the conduct of their affairs but to join their lives with one another, that is, to support one another's agency.

There has been talk these days about alternative ethical theories, those that take rights as fundamental and those that take virtues as fundamental, so that we are invited, as philosophers, to choose between "an ethics of rights" and "an ethics of virtue." But what this can possibly mean is surely unclear. Are we to derive virtues from rights or vice versa, a consideration of the virtue of generous or benevolent action, for example, from one of the rights of moral agents? Can *this* be seriously proposed? Or are we being asked to consider whether we can get along in our moral theory without any attention to rights, or, given that we focus upon rights, without any attention to virtues? One can, of course, manage to get along with all sorts of things, including insanity, but if, reasonably, we are to get along with any normative conception of moral agents, we had better take into account both rights and virtues. The virtue of conscientiousness, for example, although it may not involve any consideration of one's obligations to others, as in the case of the craftsman who is much too conscientious to do a sloppy job simply because it would be sloppy, generally does involve a consideration of one's obligations to others, and, if we are at all clear about it, of their correlative rights. Whether one is conscientious or not in meeting one's obligation (or in refusing to do so in special circumstances) surely is crucial to one's integrity as a moral agent, and it may well require the virtue of courage to do the right thing in the face of unreasonable hostility, for example, when one must take a disputed moral stand. Once more, moral agents are members of a moral community, the normative requirements imposed upon them being not only to accord or, in special circumstances, to refuse to accord one another their rights but also to act with the appropriate virtue or virtues during the course of their dealings with one another.

The current talk about ethics of virtue versus ethics of rights, like the traditional distinction between duties of perfect obligation and duties of imperfect obligation, is only one more item in the philosophical literature that should receive the interment it deserves.

4. During the course of these remarks we have reviewed a
number of considerations to which we need to advert if we
are to make a sound judgment of the degree of progress, if
any, that has been made in our moral thinking by virtue of
the conception of rights to which we have been led. The
plain fact of the matter is that no argument is needed in
order to show that we have indeed made progress. What is
needed, rather, is an invitation to review the cases and the
considerations that we have presented, with the sensitivity
and the understanding of which we are capable. But who,
it may be asked, are the "we" in question? Obviously not
those of use whose thinking about rights is as unperspica-
cious as those for whom a right is a moral note that is payable on demand. Or those for whom the requirements of
morality are laid down in a few directives issued from "On
High," to be met no matter what the circumstances may be.
If this provokes the charge of begging the question, our response must be that the demand for a proof that will be
persuasive even to those who have suffered from arrested
moral development is itself irrational. Only those who are
not only morally concerned but morally sensitive, and
thereby capable of understanding the relevant circumstances
of each case in which moral agents are involved, are in a
position to make reliable judgments about the progress that
may have been made in our moral thinking. We do not ask
the unmusical for their opinions of the worth of a musical
composition or the humorless for their views about the witty
character of a remark; and we do not ask those who are
insensitive to moral considerations for their views about
moral progress. Is it, therefore, only a matter of "you see it
or you don't," so that those who don't "see" as we do are
automatically excluded from the inner circle whose views
are to be respected? Surely not, for here, unlike the cases of
humor and music, much more can be said in explanation
and justification; but at some point explanation and justification must come to an end.

Here we need only recall what is involved in the ideal of a moral community as we have sketched it: its members are concerned with one another's well-being, and they manifest the desirability features of rights along with other moral relations with one another in their thoughts, feelings, and actions. Have we then made progress by thinking of rights in the manner advocated here? The question, if indeed it is one, provides its own answer.

5. Clearly it is our concern as members of the moral community to promote as widely as possible an understanding of the different kinds of considerations to which moral agents must attend. But does this imply that any of these must apply equally to all agents and in all situations to which they are pertinent? The question may seem absurd, for it appears to run counter to the point, made earlier in Section II of this chapter, that the very idea of a reason involves the notion of generality. And, further, it appears to contradict the thesis advocated earlier that the very idea of a moral community involves the normative requirement of a common or shared understanding of the considerations that function as moral reasons. How can a reason that applies to agents A and B fail to apply equally to both of them? And if it fails to do so, how is it possible for A and B to share an understanding of the reasons that apply to them?

Mill remarked that one would be blamed "for giving . . . family or friends no superiority in good offices over strangers" when this could be done "without violating any duty."[11] Suppose, however, that one must choose between sibling and friend in a matter that is of some importance but does not pose a tragic dilemma. Here different persons might well make different choices, depending on the importance to them of sibling and friend. A sibling might well be someone who plays a far more important role in one's

---

11. *Utilitarianism*, Chap. V.

life than anyone who might be one's friend. For in many cases a sibling is one with whom one has shared much of one's life, but a friend may be only an agreeable and helpful companion with whom one has a mutual understanding that is relatively circumscribed and superficial. In other cases, however, a friend might well be someone whose goods one has made one's own, whose joys, sorrows, successes, and disappointments one shares, in short, someone whose life has become a profoundly important part of one's own. Some might be tempted to put down this disparity to ambiguity, "friend" and "sibling" meaning different things to different persons. But this will not do; for an ambiguity once exposed can be eliminated and with it any apparent difference. In the present case, the disagreement is founded on quite subjective matters: the personalities of the persons who must choose, and the quite different ways in which sibling and friend are bound up with their own lives. There is, then, an unavoidable subjectivism in cases of this sort. And consider a relatively trivial case: if the person to whom one is bound by a promise is "touchy" about the failure to keep promises, one should be particularly careful to live up to one's word; and if circumstances make it impossible or particularly undesirable to do so, one would be well advised to take what may well be unusual steps to remedy matters.

Of course a reason, insofar as it is a reason, possesses an inherent generality: it serves as a reason in every similar situation. If one ought to help one's friend, one ought to do so whoever one's friend may be, but one's friends may be extraordinarily close, or merely casual—persons to whom one would never disclose one's innermost thoughts and feelings. And one ought to give special consideration to one's sibling, but this may not be of the same order of importance for one as the special consideration one ought to give a very close friend. Of course, the fact that the person to whom one is to give special consideration is a sibling is one good reason for doing so; and so is the fact that the person is one's friend. But the situation here is like that of our having a reason for saying p to A, namely, that it is a case of the telling of the truth. For telling the truth to A is never merely telling the truth. It may well be a case of bringing disaster upon A. So it is in the cases of giving special consideration to sibling and friend. In the former case it may be giving special consideration to one who is far more important in one's own life than any of one's friends. In the latter case the reverse may be true. It is intelligible, therefore, that differences in the choices that persons may make in the ways they are to respond to the needs of siblings and friends are the unavoidable results of subjective matters because of their personal relations with them. We not only tend, as philosophers, to think of friends and siblings in terms of stereotypes, we also are inclined to look for something pertaining to the nature of the entities we call "friend" and "sibling" to explain the choices we make, forgetting our own personal relations with them. These relations and the subjective matters involved in them render intelligible and altogether reasonable the different ways in which different persons give siblings or friends "superiority in good offices." Here it is not rules or general principles that guide us but the specific character of our own personal relations, in which quite subjective matters play their important roles.

It should now be clear how one is to reply to the second objection to our question about the considerations to which moral agents must attend. Of course membership in the moral community involves a shared understanding of the reasons to which we must appeal in the justification of the roles that rights and obligations play in our lives. But this does not mean that any given right—the right of a sibling or the right of a friend—does or should always play the same justification role, without regard to the ways in which sibling and friend are involved in our own lives. What is needed, rather, is an understanding of why the rights of sibling and friend do and should operate in various ways in the justification of conduct. This shared understanding among members in good standing of the moral community, who possess, therefore, the requisite degree of sensitivity to moral matters, involves the recognition of why one person should give "superiority in good offices" to some particular friend, whereas another should give it to sibling.

9. Solutions?

That the accounts given by philosophers of the nature of moral rights have changed since first explicit mention was made of them in very early modern times is evident. In the critical account I have given of these views, in particular those of Locke and Mill, my own views have been set in opposition to each of them. For I have criticized these views not only in the light of changes that have occurred at the popular level, as in the case of the post–World War II talk about human rights and the even more recent movements in support of the claim that even animals have moral rights, but also from my own sense of changes that need to be made in much of present-day thinking, both popular and philosophical. Following Hume no less than Mill and Prichard, much current thought divorces our concern with rights from what Hume so aptly described as the softer (some would use the word "feminine") virtues, namely, the concern with the well-being of others, and even with their need as human beings for the affection the others can give them. Talk about rights is too often associated with the sort of harsh realities encountered in legal and forensic circles, in which self-interest and the protection of one's own turf predominate. But in arguing as I have that this association must be laid to rest if the notion of a moral right is to play a viable and important role in our lives, I have put myself at odds not only with much philosophical thinking of the day but also with an important segment of common sense. This raises, among others, the question whether the goal of moral progress is to enable us, in principle, to achieve solutions to any moral problem that may arise.

What indeed is involved in the notion of moral progress? One idea, as we saw in the last chapter, is that it is possible to have a moral science. If one accepts this view, one is led to the conclusion that there must be first principles, the discovery of which would enable one to solve all our moral problems. The task of moral philosophy would then appear to be to establish a moral science, the basic principles of which would serve, in theory if not in practice, as a last and decisive court of appeal to which any of our contemporary moral problems could be referred. We should then have a moral geometry, as it were, involving principles, together with priority rules for their application, which would enable us to cut our way through the confusions in which popular discussions of some of the most troubling moral problems of our time are mired. Those who find this attractive think of moral progress, either in the individual or in society, as the development of moral attitudes and behavior that progressively conform to such fundamental principles the articulation of which constitutes the task of moral philosophy.

Now there are, among others, the following two features of scientific progress. First, solutions to scientific problems are found, however difficult this may prove to be; and once this occurs alternative views no longer need concern us. They are part of the dead past. Second, once solutions have been achieved, those who continue to reject them in the face of all of the compelling evidence that has led to them succeed only in demonstrating their own incompetence. We know that the planets move in elliptical orbits, and those who do not agree show themselves to be inept. We know that the earth is roughly spherical, and those who even now think it is flat are not taken seriously.

To what extent are there solutions of the problems that sometimes confront a moral agent concerning what ought to be done? In the vast majority of cases there are no problems; without reflection, the agent does what he ought to do. One sees someone who needs help, there are no complicating circumstances, and one acts without deliberation. There is no practical syllogism involved, there is no problem, and so the question of a solution does not arise. In other cases, there are complicating circumstances. A student who likes to chat with me about some lofty topic will be coming to my office to se me; after all, I told him I would be there to talk to him, and he cut short other activities in order to see me at the appointed time. But unexpectedly my child is seriously injured and must be rushed to the hospital. There is no time to spare and no way of reaching my student. Here, too, there is no problem about what I ought to do. But even here the past cannot be ignored; for I failed to keep my word and I owe my student an explanation. I have, after all, let him down. But once *that* is done, all is well.

But there are other cases to which we need to attend, cases in which it is by no means as obvious as in the preceding ones what it is that one ought to do. Consider a relatively trivial one: I want to contribute money for some worthy cause, but how much shall I give? Ten dollars is too little, a thousand too much. Is there some solution such that if I decide to give twenty-five dollars and someone else, whose relevant circumstances are quite similar to my own, decides to give fifty dollars, at least one of us is wrong? Each of us ought to do what each thinks right, with the usual provisos of course. For as Aristotle remarked long ago, "it is the mark of an educated man to look for precision in each class of things just so far as the nature of the subject admits."[1] And, as all of us know only too well, when judgments about what one ought to do involve speculation about an uncertain future, no neat solution is possible. In such cases one can only try to make reasonable judgments about what is likely to take place, often without any hope of making a precise

1. *Nicomachean Ethics*, Bk. I, sec. 3.

calculation of the probabilities involved; and when different moral conclusions are reached by responsible and thoughtful agents, each must (ought to) do what each one thinks must (ought to) be done. Perhaps time will tell who was right, but there was no neat solution that each could have been expected to reach and no question of the competence of those who disagree.

Much more to the point at issue are those cases in which there are serious conflicts of obligation. Consider, first, the following example. Someone has promised to take his wife to dinner and, later that night, to her favorite opera. His marriage has been shaky, but he wants to preserve it if possible. While he is at work that day in his office, an urgent matter arises that needs his immediate attention. If he stays at work that night, he risks the breakup of his marriage. If he takes his wife to dinner and the opera, he risks the loss of his job. Perhaps he was ill advised to make his promise, but he did make it, and if he breaks it, he will let her down—she has gone to considerable lengths to prepare for the evening and will suffer embarrassment if she does not go. Here we do have a problem. But is there a solution, one that settles everything nicely, so that one of the alternatives can be laid to rest as part of the dead past and such that anyone who thinks it is correct succeeds only in betraying moral incompetence?

There is not likely to be agreement about which course of action should be taken by the husband. There are those who would have him choose to stay on the job, with the idea that he could later explain and secure her forgiveness. The thought here is that the husband is far more likely to mend his fences at home than do so with an employer who is indifferent to his marital problems. But there are also those who would have him take the alternative course, the thought in this case being that matters will be too far gone to save his marriage if he breaks his promise, whereas his credit with the employer could be preserved if he leaves his job in order to save his marriage. But suppose neither of these will work—he must choose between his job and his wife—what should he do? Here again there may well be two camps, one arguing that a job, after all, is only a job, but a marriage is a marriage, and the other taking the contrary position. And there will be a division of opinion that cannot be resolved in the way that it can be, in principle, in the sciences, namely, by means of further inquiry. There are, of course, those who are predisposed to some moral theory on the ground that it can provide solutions. But besides begging the question at issue such doctrines are on their very face implausible, to say the least. I shall not repeat our objections to the utilitarianism of Mill posed earlier in this essay, objections that may seem to utilitarians, among others, to be equally question begging because of their uncritical endorsement of allegedly muddleheaded common sense. But before discussing this apparent dilemma in moral philosophy, I turn to a moral problem posed in a famous statement that is particularly striking because of the unusual moral point of view expressed by its author.

The statement in question is by E. M. Forster, who wrote during the darkest days in World II, when his country was fighting desperately to defend itself, and civilization too, against the barbarous attacks of the Nazis:

> I hate the idea of causes, and if I had to choose between betraying my country and betraying my friend, I hope I should have the guts to betray my country. Such a choice may scandalize the modern reader, and he may stretch out his patriotic hand to the telephone at once and ring up the police. It would not have shocked Dante, though. Dante places Brutus and Cassius in the lowest circle of Hell.[2]

Let us set aside circumstantial considerations that might be employed in order to resolve the difficulty in choosing between the alternatives presented, for example, that if one were to betray one's country to the Nazis, friendship itself

---

2. "What I Believe," in *Two Cheers for Democracy* (London: Edward Arnold, 1951), p. 78.

could not endure in any meaningful way. So, too, with the attempt to resolve the husband's dilemma by arguing that if he were to lose his job, he could not maintain the kind of life that would be essential to the survival of his marriage. If one considers the options simply on their own terms and without regard to extraordinary circumstances and consequences, why should one choose one rather than the other? One has an obligation to one's wife and to a company, both of which have rights or claims of some sort against one. And so it is with the choice between betraying one's friend and betraying one's country. Someone might object at this point that collectivities cannot be said to have any right against one: moral rights are the moral property of moral agents, and neither companies nor countries are moral agents. Let that be so, but it is worth mentioning that one's devotion to one's company is not the devotion to a company president one happens to despise, nor is the love one has for a country a love one has for a government or a president one happens to detest. But the problem in either case does not rest on the question whether company or country has moral rights but on the fact that the right that does exist (that of wife or friend) conflicts with another important moral consideration. And what I want to discuss now is the familiar line that is often taken in such cases: the line that the conflicts in questions are conflicts of value. For we need to ask ourselves what the conflicting values are in each of our two cases. Is the conflict in the one case between the value or worth of one's wife and that of one's job, and in the other between the values of friend and country?

The view that may be suggested by this line of thought brings to mind the attempts of Kantians to derive the rights of persons from the inner worth they have because of their status as beings endowed with rational will (ironically, an attempt Kant himself never made). Rational nature, Kant held, exists as an end in itself. But quite apart from the fact that, to borrow an expression Wittgenstein used about quite a different issue, nothing like rationality and its alleged intrinsic value or worth could possibly have the required consequences (for how can one deduce the complex variety of features of moral rights from this inner preciousness of agents independently of any relations in which they stand to others in the quite concrete circumstances of human life?). The appeal to some inner preciousness is hardly to the present issue; for the inner worth that is needed here is not something common to all human beings but something that is peculiarly present in those to whom we have quite special attachments.

Consider first the wife in our example of the husband faced by a dilemma. Does he love her for her rationality or worth? There is, after all, the case of Mildred, the unworthy and unreasonable character in Somerset Maugham's *Of Human Bondage*. And if the husband were asked about the worth or value of his wife, he might well be offended—she is not his chambermaid or the woman who takes care of the house and the children, but the woman he loves and whose life is inextricably bound to his own. And whatever may be said about the value or worth of our husband's company or of his superiors, who fully expect him to stay in his office to meet the unexpected emergency, it would be unpersuasive to argue that he had no moral obligation to do so. So, too, in Forster's example. Someone, flawed as he may be, is his friend and has every reason to expect protection from anyone to whom he is bound by the ties of affection. And, although we have supposed that one's country does not have a right against one, one does have a duty—some would call it a moral obligation—to do what one can to serve one's country in emergencies. When Nelson sent the message "England expects every man to do his duty" to the men in his fleet, this was not simply a reminder to those who had signed on as sailors in the Navy that they were bound by relevant rules, regulations, or laws to stand at their posts and obey their superior officers; it was also a call to his men to remember that they were serving a great cause. For the England in question was their home. It would be much too bland to say that betraying one's country is doing what is wrong or not expected of one.

In each of the two cases, then, there is a right, the right of a wife or of a friend, that conflicts with another important moral consideration (and whether or not the latter is itself a moral right, as we noted above, is not to the present issue). For the conflict in either of these cases is surely not merely— if it is at all—a matter of the intrinsic worth or value of wife or country (bad as she is, she is after all my wife; and imperfect as it is, it is after all my native land), and so, too, with my company and my friend. The dilemmas posed in each of these cases are not the dilemmas involved in the choice of inner or intrinsic values of wife and country, or of friend and company—values discoverable by the mind's eye as it focuses narrowly upon each of the entities in question, independently of the relations in which they stand to the victim of circumstances, namely, the person faced with the dilemma. Still less are these conflicts between the value of the rationality that human beings actually have to a greater or less degree and something else, like job or country. And certainly it cannot be the value of some metaphysically grounded rationality that all human beings have equally (that *is* whistling in the dark!) that poses the urgent problems faced by husband and by friend in the examples we have been considering. Our concern is with human beings as we find them in *this* world and in the course of the lives they live with us and others. The importance of my friend, when I weigh it against that of my country, or that of my wife when I weigh it against my job, cannot be identified with some preciousness that these entities have independently of the particular ways in which my life is bound up with them.

What then are the conflicts in values in each of these cases? Surely they must be the conflicts in the importance that wife and job have in the life of the husband, and that friend and country have in the life of anyone who must choose between betraying one or the other. If one wishes, one can say that it is the conflict between the values of one's relation to wife and job in the one case and the values of one's relation to friend and country in the other. It is this sort of importance, this sort of value, that needs to be spelled out, so I turn now to this task. The results of this undertaking will, I believe, have important consequences for the question posed in this section, namely, whether there are solutions to moral problems, and whether there are in fact fundamental principles of morality and priority rules for their application that all reasonable and sensitive moral agents might employ in any decision they reach concerning what it is that they ought to do.

Let us begin again with the dilemma posed by Forster. Most of us, perhaps, would not agree with Forster. Why this disagreement? Indeed, is it even clear *what* the alternatives are? By merely stating them as he does, Forster does not ensure that his readers will understand what might be involved. Some imagination or sensitivity, as I shall show, is required if his readers are to understand what is, or might well be, at stake.

Most readers might say that they have many friends—certainly Forster did—for there are many with whom they have friendly relations. And surely the betrayal of one's country is a much, much more serious offense than the betrayal of someone with whom one is on friendly terms. Some, undoubtedly, would be horrified at the thought of the betrayal of one's country: my country right (one hopes) or wrong (if in fact it is). Can these be the issues involved?

Consider what might be involved in a case of friendship. I am a friend of all sorts of people in my university. I would certainly not consider it incorrect for them to represent themselves as friends of mine when they introduce themselves to my wine merchant; and I have no reason to doubt that I am on such good terms with them that they would not hesitate, if I asked, to do me favors of one sort or another. I also have friendly relations with my banker such that both of us stand to benefit from our dealings with each other. But it is not these sorts of friendships that we need to consider. For what Forster had in mind are those very close personal relations in which friends lay bare their hearts—their innermost secrets, their hopes, and their aspirations—to each other, have important common interests, and are so bound to each other that they take satisfaction in each other's achievements and stand ready to help whenever necessary.[3] These are paradigm cases of close friendship, cases that are not possible with large numbers of persons each of whom in some diluted sense of the term can be said to be a friend. Will Rogers once remarked that he never met a man he did not like; this could only be said by someone whose knowledge of some persons was at best only very superficial. For any normal person to suppose that he or she could be a close friend with everyone would be irrational. For in the case of very close friends, each is not occasionally but frequently mindful of the interest of the other and so bound to the other that an offense against either one is an offense against the other. They have so joined their lives that each is saddened by the other's sorrows, takes pleasure in the other's achievements and joys, shares some measure of the grief the other suffers, and so on. No one excepts a saint could possibly be this close to most or even to many other human beings.

These are matters of which good novelists are clearly

3. In Bk. VIII of the *Nicomachean Ethics*, Aristotle uses a term commonly translated as "friendship" that is much broader in its application than this English word. For under his term he includes not only the kinds of relations I have described but also the relation between parent and child, husband and wife. Our expression "friend of the court" involves a further extension of the use of "friend," the person in question being a "friend" simply by virtue of the fact that the person is acting in the interest of the court. There is, clearly, an enormous difference between this relation and that involved in the brotherly love that Aristotle often has in mind.

aware, but that philosophers ignore when they think of friendship as a relation between persons based on sympathy together with the pleasures and pains it generates. Nor will it do to add dashes of common interest and mutual liking to establish the close friendship one finds important in one's life. There are many I like whose company I enjoy and with whom I have some common interests, but very few to whose interests as a whole I am by no means indifferent, whose lives, that is, are bound up with my own in the way I have described and whose good therefore is a matter of my own good. But friends are individuals with their own beliefs, hopes, aspirations, interests, and so on. It would be incoherent to suppose that the interests, and the goods, of friends are simply the interests and the goods that each has in common with the other. Each of one's close friends is a person in his or her own right; for to suppose otherwise is to entertain something like the impossible mirroring in the Leibnizian system of monads. The lives of close friends are different, although each is tied to that of the other. And the closer friends are to each other, the more their lives are like those of brother and sister, father and son. Small wonder that Aristotle in his discussion of the topic includes the latter in his list of the kinds of relation that translators of his text have labeled "friendship."

Contrast such closely related persons with a crowd united by some common cause. How different such friendship is, marked as it is with warm emotions, from that emotionally charged union in which, characteristically, individuality is obliterated as the members of the crowd cheer in support of the cause that brought them together. One has only to recall, if one is old enough to have lived through those times, or to see dramatically and frighteningly represented in Nazi propaganda films, the fanaticism displayed by human beings reduced to disciplined human robots, to appreciate Forster's distaste for the depersonalization of the individual into a mere member of a mass whose persuasive force is a simple function of its size. Small wonder that the sense of loneliness of a person in the midst of a crowd of passersby can be far more acute than that of someone wandering alone in the countryside!

To all of these sentiments, the response may be made that they are only subjective matters, symptoms of idiosyncratic interests and preferences. Morality, it will be said, is concerned with considerations that apply equally to all moral agents. Kant, for example, who does regard certain inclinations, to use his term, as relevant considerations in testing the validity of certain moral maxims, limits them to those that may be presumed to apply to all human beings, for example, the desire that people have for the assistance that others can provide and the need for love and sympathy. But in Forster's dilemma we are asked to consider as morally relevant the members of a multitude united by a common cause who are reduced to depersonalized, faceless beings whose individualities have been washed out of them, in contrast with the far more attractive picture of a very close friend with whom one's own life is bound in ways that render the betrayal of the friend an intolerable loss of one's own integrity as a human and moral being.

The response to this may well be that the contrast presented by this representation of the stakes involved in the choice that Forster hoped he would be able to make reflects nothing but the quite special interests and preferences of his own way of life. For granted the importance—the great value—of friendship, any member of a crowd cheering in behalf of some common cause is, after all, an individual with specific attachments to other human beings and the rights and obligations that are inseparable from the mutual understandings that exist between them. And quite apart from the unthinking patriotism of a child conditioned to salute the flag and sing a national anthem, there is a love of country which many or most of us have. For a country that one might consider betraying need not be identified in one's thoughts with a mere bit of geography, with its contemptible leaders or supine legislative body, or with a mass of people living within certain borders and using (or misusing) a common language. It may also be thought of as something much more important: as one's motherland, fatherland, or homeland with its special culture, traditions, institutions, and ideals that one has taken to heart ever since one's earliest years, and increasingly so as one's understanding has matured. It may be thought of as a land in which one has been nurtured, whose very landscapes, fields, rivers, and mountains are inseparably associated with one's own self-image. It would be a terrible, dreadful thing to have to chose between betraying one's country if all of this is what one's country means to one; it would in fact be impossible to betray a country that played such an important role in one's life without a complete loss of one's integrity. To be sure, friendship is important, and we do have friends whom we entertain and who entertain us, persons whose companionship we enjoy and strive to maintain and promote, friends with whom we consort on our holidays and friends who are close enough to us to provide for us, as we do for them, the mutual assistance that goes with friendship. But we can and sometimes do cut these ties when, for example, we move away to some distant place, and make new friends, without suffering the traumatic loss of someone whose friendship is as important as the sort of thing Forster had in mind.

Thus, dreadful as the choice may be that Forster would have liked to be able to make in the circumstances he describes, we can understand its rationale, just as we can understand why someone, whose country has played a much more important role than any friend may have done, might well choose to betray friend rather than country. Terrible as these choices may be, both are intelligible; for the stakes are different. Indeed, the two choices are between different sets of alternatives. In the one case the choice is between betraying a friend whose life is closer to one's own than any of the many so-called friends with whom there are mutual understandings, and betraying a country that is relatively unimportant in one's life. In the other the choice is between betraying a friend who is little more than an agreeable companion and betraying a country to which one is profoundly in debt. These are moral choices, tragically forced upon one and of such an order of magnitude that there must ensue an enormous burden of guilt. For even though Forster saw his countrymen, united in their cause against the Nazis, as depersonalized and unattractive human beings, this did not imply that their fate at the hands of victorious Nazis was of no concern to him. So, too, with the person whose attachment to his country is of such an order that in similar circumstances the only course he can take is to betray a companion whom he counts among his friends. Here those who differ because of the differences in the roles friends and country play in their lives cannot say to each other "Do what you think you ought to do"; for the moral costs and the burdens of guilt each must bear are far too great for either one to indulge in the use of a sentence that serves normally to express one's acquiescence in or tolerance of someone else's decision.

But it is not only in tragic circumstances such as these that subjective considerations play an important role in our moral decisions. For unlike the cases considered much earlier in our discussion, in which we do express our tolerance of decisions with which we happen to disagree because of the difference in our estimates of the consequences of actions, there are instances in which character traits often play an important role in the decisions we make. For when the stakes are not momentous but nonetheless important, personal considerations do matter. When, for example, a person decides to give mother rather than father some moderate but untrivial "superiority in good offices," as Mill put it, on the ground that she did bring one into the world and suckle one in infancy, and thereby sets aside as a matter of lesser importance the closeness of the relation to father, is there any proof that can always be given of the correctness of this choice rather than the other? Understandably, subjective considerations may well play a role in determining the weights to be given these competing alternatives.

To all of this it will be said that we have introduced a subjectivism that is antithetic to that reasonableness that characterizes the moral point of view. For in morality, some say, the considerations to which appeal must be made by reasonable agents in arriving at their decisions are considerations that apply equally to any and all moral agents. But morality is not like science, which offers us hope of achieving solutions accepted by all, deviations from which can only demonstrate incompetence. In morality there are no universally quantified principles together with priority rules for their application that ensure that there is this analogy with science. For if the integrity of a self can be secured only if moral decisions are consonant with variable subjective factors—character traits, interests, temperaments, and preferences—these cannot be dismissed as irrelevant to our moral concerns. If indeed there is subjectivism in the account given here, it is a subjectivism that must surface on occasion and without any loss of the mutual respect that is a moral desideratum. If there were capriciousness in the decisions made in the cases I have described, it would occur if the agent ignored relevant subjective considerations and decided simply by the toss of a coin. In normal cases in which I must decide, for example, whether to see one movie rather than another, and there is nothing to choose between them, I might well be reasonable in choosing by tossing a coin. But given the fact that morality plays an important role in the lives of persons in their relations with one another, the ideal of a reasonableness in which all of the varying subjective aspects of human existence are always shut off from view, is itself unreasonable.

Someone might object, however, that at best we have

shown not that there can be no solution to the problem posed by Forster but only that different persons might understandably arrive at different solutions. A solution, however, that involves the necessity of assuming a burden of guilt is hardly what one should expect a moral science to prove. For in science, once solutions are reached, any alternative that may have been considered and rejected can be put completely out of mind and consigned to the dead past. In the present case, however, there remains unavoidably the burden of guilt. It would be monstrous after deciding which to save—friend or country—to ignore as a matter of a dead past the betrayal for which one was responsible.

Further, we need to be reminded that in considering cases in which different persons understandably would be led to make different sorts of choices, we have so far considered only extreme cases of friends and country. Forster was thinking, no doubt, of a friend whose involvement in his own life was extraordinary and of a country as a bit of geography inhabited by people in none of which whom he had any particular interest. And someone who would choose to betray friend rather than country might well be thinking of a friend who is much less intimately involved in one's life and of his country as something that has shaped the character of his own being in ways that run wide and deep. But there are intermediate cases of friend and country such that there might well be no reason to give either the preference in deciding which one is to be saved, which one to be betrayed. However one might choose one would be lost; for there could be no lesser of the two possible evils, nothing right that one could do, and no possible solution to the problem.

There are ever so many different sorts of cases in which moral solutions might be, and on very rare occasions actually are, impossible. Can it reasonably be claimed, if one must choose between saving the life of one's mother and saving that of one's father, that a reasonable choice, dreadful as this might be, can always be made no matter what may be true about mother, father, and the particular circumstances of the case?

I turn, finally, to our example of the husband who must choose between wife and work. Here again, as in the problem posed by Forster, it is not clear *what* the issues are. Does he want to maintain a marriage for social appearances, to provide a home for the children he loves far more than he does his wife, to enjoy the benefits of the inheritance she will receive shortly on the death of her terminally ill father, or something else again? And does he want to keep his job because there are few employment opportunities for a person with his skills or for some other reason?

Let us then consider the following scenario. The husband has followed the normal pattern of courtship, marriage, and fatherhood, and has been a good provider. But he comes to develop a passion for painting—recall the case of Gauguin—for he discovers that he is talented, and so he simply turns his back on all of his moral commitments, leaving his family to fend for themselves while he goes off to begin a new career as an artist. Morally speaking, he should not have succumbed to his new passion by leaving his family. But we should be saddened to see someone who does have talent neglect it and remain at his job in order to live out what must now seem to him to be the humdrum existence of a morally acceptable husband and father. The choice was between doing the moral thing and venturing into a new career as an artist. Was he right after all to turn his back on his moral responsibilities?

The question is unsettling—we should like to resolve the problem by imagining that, after all, the marriage was in trouble, etc. But this is to beg the question whether there aren't cases in which, morally undesirable as certain courses of action may be, they do not warrant the simple condemnation we reserve for familiar cases of self-indulgent moral irresponsibility. For in the case under discussion, whatever loss of moral coin there may be seems to be compensated in some way by the immense gain in some nonmoral good. Who would disapprove of realizing some great artistic good at the cost of the breaking of a number of promises that are certainly not earth shaking in their importance? Certainly each of us *should*, it would seem, ignore many of the moral injuries we receive from others if these were the unavoidable consequences of the efforts expended in the production of a great work of art. And however much we might regret it, given that we are the moral agents we are, we should not simply condemn such behavior; we might in fact, and on balance, think that it was worth the loss of moral coin. But, it will be asked, where can one draw the line in measuring moral losses against nonmoral gains? The answer is that there is no line that can be drawn, for there is no arithmetic that can be employed in measuring moral and nonmoral values. And no doubt there will be no agreement whether our husband did what he should have done, not matter what his choice happened to be. It is here that people's sensibilities about considerations both moral and nonmoral (however that distinction is to be made out) are irrelevant in understandable and important ways. What *should* the husband have done in his situation? This is not a question that calls for a moral reply, but one that takes due account of, among other things, aptitudes, aspirations, and achievements that, as such, are eminently worthy of our appreciation. Are there always solutions available for all practical problems of *this* sort?

No one of us is merely a member of the moral community; we are also beings with a variety of interests, the successful pursuit of which provides diverse sorts of goods that in themselves are not moral goods, but that do contribute to lives worth living. Each of us has a right to pursue interests, but no one has any moral right to do anything that is wrong. But the husband's pursuit of his interest as an artist is also the repudiation of his obligations as husband

and parent. Are we then to adopt a rigid moralism that would condemn without reservation the violation of any right, in the absence of more compelling moral considerations? Utilitarians would answer that we should, for on such a view all goods are lumped into one basket; and, in our example, the question whether the husband acted rightly or wrongly is to be answered by ascertaining whether consequences, however remote or indirect they may be, provide a balance of goods over evils. But this is much too monolithic a moral theory. What our husband did was morally improper however greatly he may have added to the aesthetic appreciation and enjoyments of others. But since we are not only moral agents, and as such members of the moral community, but also human beings in a great many other respects, for whom, accordingly, morality cannot be the be-all and end-all of our existence, there remains the possibility—for which we do have confirming examples as in the case of Gauguin—that as rational beings, we should be prepared, in quite special cases, to set aside our moral interests and approve of what in effect are breaches of morality. If this implies that in such cases we are of divided minds, that we may not even agree concerning what it is best to do, so be it. The alternative is to trim the facts about values to the Procrustean bed of our preconceived moral philosophies.

10. Conclusions

We began this essay by raising the question whether the Greeks had any conception of moral rights, and in the course of the review of evidence provided by those who have answered in the affirmative, a number of cautions were voiced. But now, after an extensive discussion of various accounts of moral rights, including the one to which we have been led, it may be complained that we have made much too much about our initial cautions. After all, it may be said, we are prepared to accept the view that some nonhuman members of the animal kingdom have moral rights, albeit in some truncated form; why not concede, therefore, that the Greeks did have *some* notion of a moral right, incomplete as it may have been and despite the fact that there was no word for it in their moral vocabulary? The question clearly, is not whether the Greeks had moral rights, or whether those they enslaved had any moral rights—of course they did—but whether in their moral thinking there was enough to justify us in asserting that they had any such notion. And, it will be asked, don't we say that a person does have some notion of what a right is, even though in one or more respects it may be woefully inadequate? For a person may be said to have some notion of a moral right even if the notion is of something like a note that is payable on demand; and a child who has not yet completed its moral education, and who has not yet learned that there are moral burdens that go along with the moral authority it has as the possessor of rights, does have *some* notion of what a right is, abridged and even distorted as it may be. Why not, there-fore, say *tout court* that the Greeks did have *some* concep-tion of a right, although in this exceptional case they had no word for it?

To this one might add other positive evidence that so far seems to have been ignored. For there are certain moral emotions conceptually linked with our thinking about rights, such as guilt and remorse, that are appropriate to one's sense that one has violated a right. And can one reasonably sup-pose that these, along with the notions of restitution and forgiveness, notions that go with the idea of remedial mea-sures taken by wrongdoer and wronged, were unfamiliar to the Greeks? Besides, so the objector may continue, in the account given earlier, in chapter 7, of the manner of which a child might come to understand what a right is, we noted how the ground might be prepared for a child's mastery of the use of the term "a right" by his using just the sorts of items with the equivalents of which the Greeks were surely familiar: "one's own" as contrasted with "what is in one's grasp or possession," "one's due," "depriving one of one's own or one's due," "transgressing against one," etc. Further training adds to this ground—in the ways we indicated—that in these cases we say there is a right that has been exercised, respected, or violated, and so on. Why not say, therefore, that enough was present in the thinking of the Greeks to justify our believing that they did have some no-tion of a right, and that the later introduction of the new word for the moral property of a person served only as a convenient hitching post to which these locutions, with which the Greeks were clearly familiar, could be tied? Why all the fuss?

Consider, to begin with, the last objection. Of course, the introduction of a new word or expression may have no fur-ther point than to effect an economy in the use of words and perhaps in this way to facilitate our thinking. In this sort of case there is no issue of a change in concepts; for the new word is only a convenient substitute for a more lengthy and cumbersome expression. But in the present instance the case is altogether different. To say that *A* has a right to *x* (when *x* is "one's own" or some doing in which *A* might engage) is not simply translatable into a more lengthy statement about what ought to be done—the conceptual ramifications of the concept of a right as we have been at pains to set forth during the course of this essay are much too closely interwoven with the complex structure of moral discourse. It was not simply a change in vocabulary but in the character of our moral thinking that was initiated by the new talk about rights in early modern times. For now what increasingly occupies center stage is no mere set of requirements imposed upon individuals by natural or divine law but the authority or "power," as Locke and others put it, of persons not only to order their own lives but also to impose moral requirements upon others by virtue of the rights they have against them. The new term for a right thus brings together a complex set of notions in a new way, a way that brings into focus the importance of the person who as moral agent may not only order his or her own affairs but also, as the possessor of rights against others, limit or expand the permissible behavior of others.

Given all of this, it will be objected, the fact nonetheless remains that the ancients did use just the sorts of locutions the equivalents of which we employ during the course of the moral instruction we give a child, as the result of which it comes to understand what a right is. Granted that with the new moral climate of the early modern period the introduction of the talk about rights served to emphasize the importance of the freedom of the individual and his authority as the possessor of rights, still, didn't the Greeks have enough grasp of notions parallel to those *we* employ in imparting to the child an understanding of what a right is, and enough familiarity with the moral emotions connected with rights, to warrant our saying that the ground was sufficiently prepared for rights talk and, accordingly, that the Greeks had *some* grasp of what is involved in our talk about rights. Why not say that *implicitly* they did have some notion of a moral right? The new talk about rights in Locke and in his predecessors and successors marked nothing revolutionary; it was only a further and an explicit development of what was already there. So goes the reply.

The matter is not that simple, however. John Wisdom reported that Wittgenstein, during the course of his lectures in the 1930s, had raised the question whether one can play chess without the queen.[1] The queen, after all, is only one piece in the game, distinct from any of the others; and the game certainly can go on after the queen has been lost. So it looks as if all that has changed when, from the very beginning, a game is played without a queen is simply that the queen is not on the board of play. But the moves of the other pieces during the course of play are not independent of those of the queen. The queen, the most versatile and powerful piece, protects and is protected by the other pieces; in its absence the character of the game is changed as new strategies and tactics are called for, so much so that one is inclined to say that it is a different game. So too with the question, Is a game with seven cards and the deuces wild really poker? In neither case will a straightforward "Yes" or "No" answer do. But in the matter of rights, the problem is of a radically different order. Of course we use certain locutions, the presumed equivalents of which were known to the Greeks, when *we* teach a child what is involved in our concept of a moral right—locutions to which those who have claimed that "implicitly" at least the Greeks had some notion of a right have called our attention. But are we to suppose that they understood these locutions in the very same way that we do, given that they did not recognize as we do the peculiar authority of right holders over those who

---

1. *Paradox and Discovery* (Oxford: Blackwell, 1965), p. 88.

are bound to them? Are we to suppose that, in the absence
of this focus upon the freedom of the individual and the
authority that goes with it, everything else in the moral
'game,' including the use of these locutions that *we* happen
to employ in the moral education of the young, was the
same? If we may not, then the proper analogy in the case
of chess would be a change far greater than that involved
in the absence of the queen.

The suspicion that something like this is the case may well
arise on reading the brief remarks about the term "person"
that Locke himself makes during the course of his well-
known discussion of personal identity, in the *Essay Concerning Human Understanding*.[2] There, as we saw above in
chapter 8, he tells us that "person" is "a forensic term, ap-
propriating actions and their merits; and so belongs only to
intelligent agents, capable of a law, and happiness, and mis-
ery," the law in question being "the divine law . . . which
God has set to the actions of men—whether promulgated
to them by the light of nature, or the voice of revelation."[3]
But when he declares that persons are "concerned and accountable," the accountability in question is their accountability to God for their failures to abide by that divine law,
by reference to which persons and their merits are to be
judged. In quoting "the apostle" who declared that on judgment day "everyone shall 'receive according to his doings' "
and according to whatever else there may be disclosed when
" 'the secrets of all hearts shall be laid open,' "[4] Locke
clearly intends the accountability he ascribes to persons to
be their accountability to God for their failures to abide by
or conform to that law of which, as he puts it, persons are
capable. Granted that Locke's primary interest in this discussion is the consciousness of past doings as a criterion of

2. Bk. II, Chap. XXVII, sec. 26.
3. Ibid., Chap. XXVIII, sec. 8.
4. Ibid., Chap. XXVII, sec. 26.

personal identity, the fact remains that in *this* discussion there is no reference of that accountability to other persons that plays a major role in the moral view he sets forth in the *Second Treatise of Government.* For however accountable we may be to that Judge when our doings are scrutinized and the secrets of our hearts are laid open, on this latter view we are, as moral agents, accountable to those against whom we trespassed by the infringement or violation of their rights. For the rights that others have against us— whether their common natural rights or those special rights they have by virtue, for example, of the promises we have freely given them—are rights the violation of which do the *right holders* moral injury, and justify the claim that *they* have suffered moral injury and that we owe *them* the explanation or redress that this calls for. But it is precisely this matter that Locke himself ignores in the *Essay Concerning the Human Understanding,* in his account of the "forensic" character of the term "person." Not surprisingly, this is the same issue that arose in our discussion of Mill's account of rights, when we asked whether it is possible on his view to explain the simple fact he himself recognizes: that when, for example, we make promises, it is those specific persons who have accepted our promises to whom we are accountable should we fail to make good; that we injure *them,* whatever else may be true about, for instance, the well-being of mankind—and in the present instance, about our relations to God.

Consider a case that brings us much closer to the moral thinking of the ancient Greeks: Antigone must choose between abiding by "the unwritten and unchanging" law of her divinities and the edict of Creon. Here the choice is between doing what she must do as one who is subject to the law of her divinities—for she is accountable to them—and doing what she must do as a subject of Creon. But in none of this is there any issue of any right. She is accountable to the divinities—not to her brother or whatever immortal remains of him there may be—for her failure to abide by the ordinances delivered from on high.

On such a moral view there is no conception of the authority or power of moral agents, which stems from their status as the possessors of rights, to order their own lives and to limit the permissible freedom of action of others during the course of their dealings with them. The moral requirements for them are summed up in the laws imposed upon them by their divinities; and they are accountable for what they do, not to one another by virtue of any authority *they* may have as moral agents, but to the divinities themselves, to whose will they must bow.

Does it make any sense on this moral view to speak of what is one's own, one's due, what one owes someone, trust, guilt, remorse, etc.? Of course it does, but the sense is quite different from that which *we* understand when these forms of speech are employed during the course of *our* talk about rights.

When, time after time, Hannibal was told by his father that the Romans could not be trusted, the point was not that they could not be counted on to meet their obligations to others, that is, to recognize and abide by the rights of those whom they were bound, but rather that it would be folly to suppose that they would abide by the "unwritten and unchanging" laws of the gods. They deserved moral condemnation for their moral offenses, but the moral offenses in question were offenses against the gods; and those who suffered because they assumed that the Romans would abide by this law had themselves to blame for thinking that when the Romans gave them their word, they would go on to act in the way ordained by their gods and by those of the Carthaginians. For when Carthaginians gave their word, they spoke in the presence of their gods, swearing an oath to *them*; and when the wretched Romans failed to keep their word, then, like Hobbes's misbehaving sovereign whose sin was to God, not his subjects—for he was not party to the social covenant—they sinned against the gods. It was not the Carthaginians who suffered the *moral* injury, however much they may have suffered in consequence of the breach of divine law by the Romans and the defeat of their expectations that the Romans would abide by that law. No doubt the Romans violated the laws of their own divinities as well as those of the Carthaginians, and on this ground alone deserved the condemnation and the retaliations that were visited upon them; but if there were beings to whom they were accountable because of their moral offenses, it was the gods in whose presence they had given their solemn oaths, and not those persons they may have hurt.

Further, what are we to make of the talk by the Greeks about what they owed one another or about someone's due? When Plato introduces Polemarchus to express the view that justice is giving each one his due and then has Polemarchus explain this as helping friends and harming enemies, he probably did voice the relic of an old siege-mentality conception of morality that could be found even in his own day. And if justice consists in abiding by the "eternal and unwritten" law of the gods, then one will give others their due if one obeys the gods. For this law requires that one help those in need, help those to whom we have given our word that we would help them, care for one's children, obey one's father, etc. But giving someone his due is *not* meeting one's obligation to him, that is, giving him that to which he has a right against one; it is simply doing what one ought to do. For, as we have seen in our discussion of Mill's view, what may be one's due, where the notion of a right is involved, may be the providing of a good to someone else (as when X promises Y to care for Y's aged mother), in certain cases to the very person who is under the obligation (as when a husband promises his wife to eat more nutritious lunches). Here it is that the very conception of a person as a moral agent is of crucial importance. For such an agent is a person who is prepared to enter into moral relations with others by virtue of which he or she supports their agency, as they do his or hers, and who exercises the moral authority and bears the moral burdens involved in the rights and obligations that constitute the moral relations in which he or she stands to them. This, clearly, is not the same thing as the conception of an agent who is simply required by divine law to provide goods for, or to receive them from, others.

So it is with locutions such as "one's own," "guilt," etc., which *we* use during the course of the instruction we give the young in order to impart to them what is involved in that concept of a right that *we* employ in our own moral thinking. On the view that the moral thing consists in conformity with divine law—a view in which there is no notion of accountability to other agents and hence no conception of a moral right—the sense of these locutions is quite different from that which *we* attach to these locutions. If there is to be an analogy of chess without the queen, we must think of the change resulting from the absence of the queen as no mere change in tactics and strategy but a change in the very moves that the other pieces on the board are permitted to make; but in that case the game, certainly, would no longer be chess. It would be a serious blunder, therefore, to assume, because these locutions were employed in antiquity, that the ancients had any concept of moral rights.

Does this mean that the Greeks had no notion of *any* sort of what a right consists in? Certainly not. All that has been shown so far is that *if* the moral thinking of the Greeks had consisted simply in the observance of divine law in their thought and action, they would have had no conception of a moral right, a conception that focuses upon the authority of persons as moral agents to deal with one another in ways that are characteristic of those who possess not only the fundamental rights that any moral agent has but also those special rights against others possessed by virtue of the mutual understandings that exist between them. This latter picture of the moral life is quite different from that of agents who are capable of a law, as Locke put it, and accountable to their Maker for their breaches of that law. When, therefore, we speak of the Greeks, for example, and debate whether or not they had any conception of a moral right, which Greeks are we talking about? The Greeks Plato had in mind when he has Polemarchus stating one popular view about the nature of justice, namely, the view of those peasants for whom the moral conduct of Homeric legend represented models of moral behavior? Or those who, like Antigone, could not take seriously the view that the "unwritten and unchanging" divine law could be the laws of the deities of popular legend who disported themselves in all-too-human fashion? Or perhaps those relatively few well-educated Greeks, if such there were, who not only did not accept as literal truth the stories about the gods and had some inkling of the moral equality of all men, free or enslaved, and of the authority of persons to order their lives in their dealings with one another, and out of their own resources as moral agents?

No doubt the Greeks did have an understanding of what was involved in the ownership of property: that it could be acquired, put to use to serve their own purposes, given away, sold, or bequeathed. And some of them certainly understood that the privileged members of their city-states enjoyed certain liberties. Does this mean, therefore, that the Greeks did have not only a conception of political and legal rights but a conception of moral rights as well? There is a danger here in reading into the evidences cited the understanding *we* have of what is involved in *our* notions of political and legal rights, a danger comparable to the one we find in our tendency to anthropomorphize in the explanations we give of the behavior of relatively primitive forms of animal life. Consider, to begin with, the alleged right of a member of the ruling class in the Greek city-state to acquire, possess, transfer, or bequeath his property. Is it being claimed that *in addition* to the notion of membership in the privileged class—the notion of citizenship—there was the notion of the rights such citizens could enjoy? Is it clear that, in saying that a member of the ruling class could own property, one was doing anything more than setting forth what was involved in being a member of the ruling class, this being explicable wholly in terms of what persons were required or permitted by statute or custom to do?

But our own idea of a political right is one that involves a good deal more. Political and legal rights, we think, are inherently subject to appraisal, criticism, and, if need be, modification, in the light of prevailing social policy and our basic moral thinking about the rights of individuals. A man's property is his own. But if I have been threatened by someone who now sets out to maim or kill me, and I am denied the opportunity by my neighbor to escape by making use of his car, on the ground that it is *his* car and therefore he can do what he wills with it, I can claim damages from him if I suffer bodily harm as the result of his churlish refusal to grant me the use of his property. For I do have a right to my life and he, an obligation to permit me to save it, even at the expense of his wishes in the matter. There are, then, provisos in our ascriptions of legal and political rights, provisos that involve matters of moral rights of which, however, the Greeks may have been quite insensible. But, further, moral rights, unlike political and legal rights, depend for their existence not upon established customs and practices but upon the status of persons or moral agents, who *as such* are in a position of authority to order their own lives in their dealings with one another. On this score, accounts of moral rights given in the past have often been unsatisfactory. But those who, like Locke, have waffled on this matter by invoking the law of nature, thereby seeking to make their own views palatable to their readers by appealing to a venerable theory of Natural Law, nonetheless did think that in

ascribing moral rights to human beings they were recognizing the authority of moral agents no less than the requirements imposed upon them. And this is quite a different matter from the authority of laws, human or divine, or the
customs or institutions of one's society, and the capacity of
agents to abide by them.

Whether any of the Greeks had any such conception of
moral agency, without which it would make no sense to
speak of moral rights, is so far unproven. In order to support
the view that the Greeks did have *some* notion of a moral
right, further inquiry is needed by historians and linguists
with the requisite philosophical skills and sensibilities that
would enable them to avoid the conceptual pitfalls we have
been at some pains to expose. But this combination of talents and skills is in short supply. It still remains to be seen,
therefore, whether any Greeks had any sort of notion of a
moral right.

Index

Accountability, to God and to other right-holders, 142–143. *See also* Antigone

Animal rights, 51–72

Animals, change in our attitude toward, 51–53, 72n; criticism of ascription of rights to many, 59–63; Hume on treatment to be given, 52; reasons some have given for ascribing rights to, 59 ff.

Antigone, 143–144

Appeal to rights, not to be identified with appeals to standards of conduct, 81

Aristotle, 121; does not mention rights in discussing justice, 1; on friendship, 128n, 129

Atkinson, Nancy, x

Bandman, B., 6n

Bentham, J., unlike Mill denies that there are *any* moral rights, 41

Berlin, I., 6n

Betrayal, of friend and country, 123–135

Blackstone, 7

Borderline cases, of ascription of rights, 67–72

Brandt, R. B., 13n

Buchanan, Allen, x, 64n

Caring, contrasted with having sympathetic feelings, 21–22, 105–116

Character traits, relevant to moral decisions, 25, 132–135

Chaucer, 4

Chess without Queen, 141, 146; contrasted with morality without rights, 141–149

Conflicts, of moral and non-moral matters, 135–137; of obligations, 122–135

Conflicts of interest, inevitability of, 98–101

Conscientiousness, of craftsmen need not involve any moral obligation, 113; of moral agent, generally a moral virtue that involves rights, 113

Constitutional rights, analogy between human and, 48–49; and doctrine of original intent, 47–55 (*see also* Dworkin, R.); fundamental and derived, 48–50; inherent generality of statements of fundamental, 47–55

Country, betrayal of one's, 123–135

Culpability, and mental disease, 110

Dante. *See* E. M. Forster

Daube, D., 1n, 2–5 passim

Demosthenes, 2

Deserving good and evil, 16

Desirability features of rights, 87–89

Due, one's, 2–5 passim

Duties of perfect and imperfect obligation, explained, 15–16; criticized, 23. *See also* Kant; Prichard

Duties to animals, 52

Dworkin, Ronald, 48n

Ends in themselves, Kant's view of, 55–57

Equality, rights and, 56–57; treating humans and animals on terms of, 57
Ethics of rights and ethics of virtue, inherent absurdity of, 113

Fairness, rights and, 56
Flanagan, T., 1n
Forgiveness, 26–28
Forster, E. M., conception of persons united by a cause, 129–130; conception of a friend, 127–127; and Dante on friendship, 123; dilemma posed by, 123–124; issues involved in disagreements with, 131–132. *See also* Friends
Friend, betrayal of a, 123–135
Friends, indefinitely many sorts of, 127–130; 'values' of, contrasted with values of involvement in, lives of others, 127–130. *See also* Aristotle

Gaugin, case of, 135–137
George V, hunting record achieved by, 52
Golding, M., 6n, 7n
Gothic, moral attitudes, 88
Guilt, 81

Hannibal, 144. *See also* Moral injury
Happiness, 90
Hart, H. L. A., 6n, 31
Hitler, 97
Hobbes, 6n, 144
Hooker, "the judicious," 11, 103, 106
Human rights, 39–50; distinction between fundamental and derivative, 47–50; inherent generality of statements of fundamental, 47–50; not forfeitable by Dr. Jekyll or Mr. Hyde, 85. *See also* Constitutional rights; Natural rights; *The Universal Declaration of Human Rights*
Hume, D., conscientious regard for promises not a "softer virtue" according to, 21–23, 119; description

of "the poetical fiction of the golden age," 98; on sympathy, 105–106; on treatment to be accorded animals, 4, 52. *See also* Caring; Conflicts of interest
Humpty Dumpty, 64

Imperfect obligations. *See* duties of perfect and imperfect obligation
Implicit notion of a right, 140–142
Inanimate objects, recent ascription of rights to, 58; reasons that have led some to ascribe rights even to, 59
Individualism, in Locke, 104–106; meaning of, 106–109
Infants, possession of rights by, 70, 83–87
Interest, inevitability of conflicts of, 98–101
Intrinsic value, allegedly possessed by all sentient creations, 57; G. E. Moore' s conception of, 57; national nature and, 55–57
Intuitionism about rights rejected, 76–79

Justice, its connection with rights (*see* Mill); Platonic conception of, 100; without rights in views of Plato and Aristotle, 1; as understood in Homeric Greece, 147

Kant, I., makes no mention of rights in his account of fundamental principles of morality, 40n; Mill's comments on Kant, 19n–20n; obscurities in view that national nature is an end in itself, 55–57; place in tradition of natural law, 22–23; treatment of inclinations, 130; why any intelligible notion of an end in itself cannot serve as a ground for ascription of rights, 53–57
Kantian, attempts to deduce rights from values, 124–126

Leibniz, 100

Liberties. *See* Rights

Locke, x, 6, 7, 8–12, 73, 75, 84, 91, 97, 119, 140; account of forgiveness, 27–28, 81; contrast between moral views in *Essay* and *Treatise*, 142–143; doctrine not egoistic, 10–12, 103–104; does not identify rights with liberties, 8, 9–10; identification of law of nature with reason, 10; individualism, 104–109; on law of nature and rights, 10–12; no sense of rights of poor against affluent, 109–110; not a libertarian, 41; notions of accountability in the *Essay* compared with that of Mill, 142–143; protectionist character of rights, 108; on right to punish, 39–41; on rights in state of nature vs. those in civil society, 9–10; sense in which natural rights are fundamental, 39–41, 53; senses in which his natural rights are absolute, 41, 41n–42n

Mabbott, J. D., 21
McClosky, H. J., 52n
Maugham, Somerset, 135
Mental disease, and culpability, 10
Midgley, Mary, 60n
Mill, J. S., x, 53–55 passim, 64, 73, 77, 115, 116, 119; account of equality and impartiality, 17; comparison of view of accountability with that of Locke in *Essay*, 143; concessions to common sense, 16–18; connects rights only with duties of perfect obligation, 15–16; definition of a moral right, 20; exposition and examination of his account of rights, 15–38; failure as utilitarian to meet own criterion that there are assignable persons who are wronged, 32–35; fatal defect in account of rights, 35–38; how mere injury becomes moral injury according to, 32–35; individualism, 111; makes no mention of natural or human rights, 39; moral rules and moral resentment according to, 19–20; not an act-utilitarian, 17 (*but see* 19–20); positive account of justice, 18–20; recognition of importance of moral rights, 14; recognizes connection of certain rights with mutual understandings, 17–18; recognizes that injustice is wronging some assignable person or persons, 18; some defects in news on promises, 111–112; view of relation of justice and rights, 15–16

Miranda case, and claim of constitutional right of an accused to remain silent, 47–48

Moral agents, as social beings, 112

Moral calculation and moral geometry, 75n. *See also* Moral geometry

Moral community, ideal of, 102; nature of members of, 102–103; need to broaden conception of rights of members of, 108–109; need to widen conception of membership of, 109–110; willingness to support agency of others a criterion of membership in, 112

Moral dilemmas, 122–135; as conflicts of values, 124–127; disagreements about, 127–135; Mill's utilitarianism and, 123

Moral geometry, 120–135

Moral ideal, 90–118; moral progress and 90–118; not an optimal state of goods and evils, 102; not to be identified with absence of all possible conflicts, 98–101; Plato's conception of, 92; utilitarian conceptions of, 90

Moral injury, Mill's view of, 32–35; how understood by Antigone and Hannibal, 143–144

Moral principles: how to understand their generality, 95–96; not universally quantified general propositions, 95–96; *prima facie* and simpliciter, 92–97. *See also* Ross, W. D.

Moral problems, and solutions, 120–
  137
Moral progress, idea of, 90–118
Moral reasons, may apply unequally
  to different agents, 115–118; inherent generality of, 116–118
Moral science, very possibility of a,
  120–137
Mutual understandings, relation of
  these, implicit or explicit, to rights
  in Mill's account, 17–18

Natural rights, Locke on, complexity
  of conceptual features of, 53–54.
  See also Human rights
Neo-Kantians, confusion about mean-
  ing of assertion of rights by, 81
North, H., 2n

Obligation-meeting acts and goods
  they provide, 28–32
Occam, William of, his conception of
  natural rights, 6–7; 91
One's due, in Plato's account of Homeric view, 2, 145; how understood
  in antiquity, 145
One's own, its sense in absence of a
  conception of moral rights, 146
Owe, and rights, 3–5

Parents, and obligation to children,
  23–24
Paul, A., 1n
Persons, as social beings, 104; as de-
  personalized beings in crowds and
  Nazi rallies, 129–130; Locke's con-
  ceptions of, 142–143
Pets, ascription of rights to, 65–71
Plato, 1, 2, 67n, 74, 90, 92, 145–147
Polemanchus, and sense in which he
  understood "one's due," 145–147
  passim
Political rights, 2; conceptual connec-
  tion with moral rights, 147–148
Prichard, 23, 88, 95, 111, 119
Prima facie duties, principles, obliga-
  tions and rights: confusions in-

volved in talk about *prima facie*
  rights, 97; motives for talk about,
  92–93; paradoxical nature of talk
  about different senses of moral
  terms, 94–97. *See also* Moral principles; Ross, W. D.
Progress, has been achieved in thinking about rights, 114–115; in morals and science, 120
Promises: authority and burdens of
  both promisers and promisees, 24–
  28; cases of first-person promises
  and goods provided by keeping
  them, 29–31; cases of third-person
  promises and goods provided by
  keeping them, 31–32; contrasted
  with debts, 24; degenerate cases of,
  28; and forgiveness, 26–27; Locke
  nowhere attempts to explain how
  rights are created by, 107–108; mutually beneficial exchange of goods
  not provided by first-persons and
  third-person, 112; one criticism of
  Hume on, 21–23; usual cases of,
  28; why they should be kept, 37–
  38
Property, physical possession vs. ownership of, 1; how acquired according to Locke, 107; how linked with
  rights in our understanding of the
  concept of, 148–149; how understood by ancient Greeks, 147–149;
  its extended meaning in Locke, 107
Punishment, right to impose it, according to Locke, 39–41

Rawls, John, 40n; conception of human rights, 44–45
Repentance, 27–28
Respect, allegedly due any living creature, 57
Rights: borderline cases of possession
  of, 67; complexity of conceptual
  features of, 53–55; in competitive
  situations, 85n; defects in earlier accounts of, 103–113; degrees of,
  67–68; desirability features of, 87–

89; distinguished from liberties, 84–85; equality and fairness need not involve, 56–57; forfeiture of fundamental rights by Dr. Jekyll and Mr. Hyde, 85; how one might acquire concept of, 76–79; inanimate objects as bearers of, 58; intuitionism in conception of, 76–79; legalism in conceptions of, 119; moral relation involved in possession of, 35–38; needs, interests and desires do not establish possession of, 57–58; no set of necessary and sufficient conditions for possession, 76, 79–89; Platonism in thinking about, 75–89; possession by infants, 83–87; progress in thinking about, 114–115; reasons advanced to support claim Greeks had a notion of, 138–149; recent revivals of interest in, 13–14; some assignable person always involved in violation, 18; variety of moral considerations other than rights as grounds for action, 58. *See also* Human rights; Natural rights

Rogers, Will, 128

Ross, W. D., moral principles patterned after scientific principles by, 92–97

Sachs, David, 2n

Santas, Gerasimos, x

Schiller, Friedrich, 22n

Shame, 27, 81

Singer, Marcus G., 13n

Slippery slope argument, 68–72

Stereotypes, in moral thinking, 117

Subjective factors, moral relevance of, 130, 132–135; moral relevance of

distinguished from capriciousness, 133

Sympathy, caring contrasted with, 21–22, 105–106

Ulpian, 1–2

Universal Declaration of Human Rights: distinction between fundamental and derivative human rights, 49–50; inherent generality of statements of fundamental human rights, 47–50, 53; list of human rights, 43; problem posed by some rights listed, 43–45; relation between certain human rights and conditions necessary for enjoyment, 49–50; some on its list not dependent simply on common human nature, 43–44. *See also* Constitutional rights; Human rights; natural rights

Utilitarianism, its failure to take proper account of moral agency, 35–37

Vegetarianism, 59, 64–65

Villey, Michel, 6n

Violation of rights, no more cause for shame, 81

Vlastos, G., 2n

Whales, changes in treatment of and in responses from, 71–72

Wildinson, Elizabeth N., 22n

Willoughby, L. A., 23n

Wisdom, John, 141

Wittgenstein, 124–125, 141

Wordsworth, 23n

Worry, nature and relevance of worry to agency, 29–32

Designer:	U. C. Press Staff
Compositor:	Auto-Graphics, Inc.
Text:	11/13 Sabon
Display:	Sabon
Printer:	Braun-Brumfield
Binder:	Braun-Brumfield